Dave & Mick's

POMPEY POP PIX

An Illustrated History of '50s & '60s Popular Music in Portsmouth

Dave Allen & Mick Cooper

© Copyright 2011 Dave Allen & Mick Cooper

All rights reserved. No part of this publication may be reproduced, stored in a retrieval system, or transmitted, in any form or by any means, electronic, mechanical, photocopying, recording, or otherwise, without the written prior permission of the author.

First Published in 2011 by Moyhill Publishing

A CIP catalogue record for this book is available from the British Library.

ISBN 978-1905597-29-1

Printed in UK

The papers used in this book were produced in an environmental friendly way from sustainable forests.

Moyhill Publishing
Suite 471, 6 Slington House,
Rankine Rd., Basingstoke, RG24 8PH, UK.
Order online at *www.pompeypop.com*

Dedication

To everyone who was there - whether you remember or not –
and to anyone else who wishes they had been.

Acknowledgements

We'd like to thank everyone who has contributed to this project in any way whatsoever but perhaps particularly Linn Beacon, Jon Bishop, Sue Butler, The Cadillacs, Geoff Collinge, Linda & John Du Pret, Phil Freeman, Roger Freeman, Nigel Grundy, David St John, Chris Harvey, the Honeys, Ken Howell, Trevor Jones, Frank Kelly, Pat Kemp, Alan King, Dave Mussell, Julie Nash, Penny Perfect, Dave Pittard, David Quinton, Tony Ransley, Colin Read, the Renegades, Phil Shulman, John Stedman, Brian Salt, Lawrie Tippins, Dorothy Wenham, Peter White, Alan Williams, Colin Wood and David Cronin of Moyhill Publishing.

For corrections, apologies and updates to the book please check the Pompey Pop Blog at http://pompeypop.wordpress.com

Photographs

45 single bag	79	Challengers and van	94
Absence on the common	149	Challengers reunion 2010	165
Academy, The	126	Cherry Smash 1967	143
Acker Bilk at the Savoy 1960	22	Chiz Bishop Quartet 1956	14
Adam Faith at Portsmouth Guildhall	62	Chris Barber Guildhall Programme	30
Alan Christmas & Rod Watts	171	Cilla and Jimmy James at the Birdcage	78
Alan, Linn & others	172	Clarence Pier Ballroom	43
Alf Hallman & his Orchestra 1956	9	Classics	102
Apache	140	Classics	101
Arthur Brown, Portsmouth Guildhall	153	Classics support David Bowie	101
Arthur Ward Band at Clarence Pier 1960s	10	Classics support Manfred Mann	101
Arthur Ward Band with pianist Bill Cole	8	Classics with Toney Ransley on vibes	95
Aubrey Small	160	Cliff & Honeys on tour	39
Aubrey Small at the Pier	160	Coastliners	103
Audrey Jeans	71	Coat design	140
Avengers at Oak Park School	57	Cobden Arms	45
		Coconut Mushroom	144
Barry & the Strollers	67	Coconut Mushroom at the Tricorn	145
Barry & the Strollers	68	Colours; Sinah Warren	152
Barry & the Strollers	85	Concorde at Kimbells	92
Barry & the Strollers at Cosham	68	Country Folk	106
Barry & Zodiacs	103	Country Joe & Reet Petite & Gone, 2001	164
Barry McCarthy & his Dixielanders 1955	23	Cresta Bob & Dave 2010	168
Barry McCarthy & his Dixielanders 1956	23	Crestas	46
Barry Roberts & Ted Wenham	105	Crimson Ballet	140
Beatles fan	65		
Benny Freedman Orchestra	13	Dance of Words ticket	142
Benny Freedman Orchestra	5	Dancing at Ricky's	42
Bernie Fox of Blues Convention	142	Dancing at Ricky's Club	28
Bert Parker & Peter Hicks	21	Dancing at the Savoy	5
Bill Haley at Portsmouth Guildhall	18	Danny Raven & Renegades 1959	53
Birdcage Mods	118	Danny Raven & Renegades reunion 2011	165
Black Cats 1964	134	Dave Pittard Mod drummer	103
Black Sabbath at the Pier	154	Demons skiffle group	27
Blackout	134	Denver Four	32
Blackout 1965	135	Derek Sarjeant	107
Blackout on stage	134	Donna & Small	109
Blackout with dance duo Crimson Ballet	135	Donna & Steve '69	116
Bobby Collins	79	DP as 'Tommy Steele'	21
Bonzo's Viv Stanshall at the Pier	158	Dynachords	87
Brave New World, Christmas 1967	139	Dynamos 1962	90
Brian Kemp of Five-by-Five - Pompey's Paul?	64	Dynamos 1963	90
Brother Bung at the Indigo Vat	141	Dynamos 1964	90
Brother Bung at the Indigo Vat	142	Dynamos on ITV's Ready Steady Win	90
Brothers Scarlett	86		
Brothers Scarlett at Hillside Youth Club	86	Eastney's Birdcage	119
Brothers Scarlett start out	33	Edgar Broughton Band, the Pier	154
Brothers Scarlett win at the Savoy	86	Empress site	174
Cadillacs	35	Family at Brave New World	155
Cadillacs at Court School of Dancing	36	Festival of Dance Music 1956 poster	4
Cadillacs NY Eve '59 Hillside Youth Club	36	First IOW Festival Ticket	80
Cadillacs, Renegades Mick & two Daves, 2010	167	Flyposting Ernie, Sears of the Rendezvous	92
Cadillacs, Renegades, Dynamos, 2010	167	For-Tunes	51
Challengers	94	For-Tunes at Ricky's	52

ii *Photographs*

For-Tunes at the Old House at Home	52
For-Tunes Josie Franklyn	51
For-Tunes reunion	168
Frank Hurlock singing at the Railway	107
Frank Kelly	47
Frank Kelly	79
Frank Kelly & Hunters	47
Frank Kelly & the Crestas	46
Frank Kelly & the Digger Hart Combo	50
Frank Kelly & the Hunters 1959	48
Frank Kelly in the mid '60s	48
Frank Kelly mid '60s	50
Freemen	42
Furys	60
Furys	61
Furys & Carnival Queen	89
Furys at St Edmunds School	61
Gary Hayman Trio	16
Generation	161
Gentle Giant at Trident Studios, London	156
Geoff, Spliff, DP	21
George Turner manager of the Savoy	14
Getting ready at the Railway	22
Gilbey Twyss	161
Ginger Baker with his Airforce at the Pier	155
Gold Dust	134
Gold Dust card	134
Graham Leslie & his Orchestra 1956	11
Groovy chicks	119
Guildhall now	44
Guildhall opens 1959	44
Guildhall organ	45
Guildhall Square	44
Harlem Speakeasy	79
Harlem Speakeasy	138
Harlem Speakeasy at the Red Door Club	138
Hayling on a sunny Sunday	82
Hayling's Russ Sainty with Cliff	173
Headline News	39
Heaven	150
Heaven Mark 2 of Brass Rock LP	151
Heaven on stage	149
Heaven recording at Southern Sounds	150
Helen Shapiro with Dave	170
Hells Angels benefit Waterlooville	149
Hendrix and Floyd at the Guildhall	80
Herbie Goins at the Birdcage	118
Hi Fis	20
High Society	162
HM Royal Marines 1955 - Dance Orchestra	11
Holiday snap	122
Honey's tour with Helen Shapiro	64
Honeys	38
Honeys	40
Honeys & Adam Faith	41
Honeys & Bobby Vee	40
Honeys & Cliff	38
Honeys 2009	166
Hot Rods	32
Hot Rods	33
Idle Race at South Parade Pier	157
Image	139
In Grandma's Absence	149
In the Audience	149
Inspiration	125
Inspiration	138
J Crow Combo	103
Jack Bruce and Manfred Mann	115
Jamie's Kin	137
Jamie's Kin at Kimbells	137
Jamming at Ricky's	29
Jazz at the Railway Hotel	43
Jimmy James & the Vagabonds	119
John Clarke celebrates his birthday	170
John Crow & Russ Hatchard	103
John Lytle of Rosemary	148
John Pounds Youth Club	20
Johnny Lyne Band	8
Johnny Lyne Band in Melody Maker	6
Johnny Lyne Band in Melody Maker	7
Johnny Preston with Tony Crombie, 1960	19
Johnny Rocco & the Paramounts	53
Johnny Rocco & the Rebels	56
Jon Isherwood	108
Jon Isherwood & Ted Wenham	105
Jon Isherwood with Terry Shulman	116
Julie Driscoll, Portsmouth Guildhall	156
Junior Twist Savoy	66
Kid Martyn Band at the Rendezvous	24
Kimbells membership 63	93
Kimbells site	174
King's Theatre	176
Klimaks	126
Klimaks at the Shoreline Club	126
Klimaks' Graham Barnes	126
Liddell Sisters mime act	16
Light Program lightshow	146
Lightshow	146
Linn - 'The Bird' DJ	141
Live Five at the City Museum 2010	166
Live Five in the movie Expresso Bongo	37
Long John Baldry	110
Long John Baldry at the Railway	109
Lyne's rhythm section	8
Manfred Mann	114
Manfred Mann on Ready Steady Go, 1964	115

Entry	Page
Manor Court	122
Manor Court ticket	137
Mark Barrie Four	127
Mick & Mrs Glover - Gill Hutchins (Crestas)	36
Mick Glover Group	37
Mick, Phil Shulman and Dave	171
Mike Devon & Diplomats	74
Mike Hugg in Abbey Rd Studio	114
Mike King	69
Morgan's Camel Train	127
Mushroom	162
Mustangs	33
Nat Gonella tribute in Gosport	30
Nigel Grundy	153
Nigel's Press Pass	153
Nights out	54
Oasis Club card	123
Oddfellows site	174
Original Strangers	53
Parkas 1967	136
Parkas' First Gig	136
Pat Nelson	106
Pat Nelson & Jon Isherwood	104
Paul Spooner at Ricky's	52
Penny	146
Pete Stanley & Wizz Jones	110
Pete Stroller & Drifters at Clarence Pier	85
Pete Stroller & the Drifters	85
Pete White	33
Peter White's 1962 'Strat' from Bennett's	74
Pevensey Brown Melon	142
Phil Freeman, Image, at Tricorn Xmas party	151
Phil Shulman	83
Pink Floyd in the Pier's Dressing Rooms	157
Portsmouth City Museum 2010	172
Railway Folk Club	111
Railway Hotel	22
Railway Hotel	104
Railway Hotel site	175
Railway regulars	112
Rampant	125
Reginald Bannistra Band 1957/58	9
Reginald Bannistra & his Music 1955	10
Rendezvous Card	92
Rendezvous poster	92
Renegades	58
Renegades	58
Renegades 1961	71
Residents 1961	58
Residents at Eastney Modern School	59
Residents rehearse at Copnor Sec Mod	59
Residents' holiday in sunny Spain	60
Ricky's Club Goldsmith Avenue	28
Ricky's site	175
Rikki Farr, MC at the IOW Festival 1970	84
Rivals 1972 Pier's Gaiety Bar	164
Rivals on ITV	56
Rivals' singer Gren Mayes	137
Robin Beste of the Birdcage	119
Rock & Roll review Sept 1956	19
Rod - Ladies Mile	98
Rod Stewart & Emmett Hennessy -	99
Rod Stewart & Robby, Osborne Rd	97
Rod Stewart ('Banjo' Rod) Southsea Common	98
Rod Stewart and pals in Pompey	97
Rod Stewart Ticket	99
Rod's autograph	99
Ron Bennett & the Club Quintet 1955	13
Rosemary	148
Rosemary at the Art College	148
Rosemary at the common Free Concert 1969	148
Royals	87
Royd Rivers & Gerry Lockran	112
Saints	26
Saints at Somerstown Youth Club	25
San Cella Sound & Rikki Martin	143
Sandie Shaw at Portsmouth Guildhall	63
Sandy Denny and Fotheringay at the Pier.	158
Saturday afternoon outside Verrecchias	96
Savoy Buildings	4
Savoy site	173
Savoy Ticket	135
Scooter boy	118
Semi Tones	57
Signed for the Liddells - Dickie Valentine	17
Simon Dupree & the Big Sound	129
Simon Dupree & the Big Sound	130
Simon Dupree & the Big Sound	131
Simon Dupree including Elton John	84
Smiling Hard	163
Snake Pit, Southsea beach	95
Sons of Man	93
Sons of Man at the Pier	93
Soul Society - The (original)	128
Soul Society at the Tricorn	128
Soul Society entertain the students	128
South Parade Pier 1950s	22
South Parade Pier 1950s	72
South Parade Pier and Savoy Buildings	3
South Parade Pier Summer Programme	15
Southern Counties Old Time Orchestra 1955	3
Southern Sounds	66
Southern Sounds	87
Southern Sounds at Ricky's Club 1962	57
Southern Sounds at the Guildhall	45
Springhill	163
St Louis Checks	123

St Louis Checks in Melody Maker	122
St Louis Checks' Chris West	124
St. Louis Checks, Rock Gardens Pavilion	124
Storms	100
Storms going to Germany	100
Strollers	69
Sue's autographs	65
Talbot Hotel	104
Talismen	88
Talismen Final	89
Talismen win Record Mirror	88
Tangerine Slyde	147
Tangerine Slyde at Stweek (Rag Week)	147
Tea Chest bass	26
Teapots	132
Teapots at Kimbells with Dorreen Parsons	132
The Action at the Birdcage	118
The Birdcage	77
The Boys at South Parade Pier	57
The Monk at the Brook Club	127
The Monk in the Rock Gdns	127
The Third Dimension 1965	87
Theatre Royal	19
Theatre Royal Programme Sept 1956	19
Theatres Orchestra 1955, Combined	12
Thunderclaps	25
Thunderclaps	27
Tipner Greyhound Stadium Festival 1970	152
Tony & Gill in Paulsgrove	20
Tony Porter	46
Travis Raymar	128
Tremors	34
Two Parkas & Trevor	169
Two Strollers	169
Vieux Carre at the Rendezvous Club 1960	24
Vocaltones & Carroll Levis at the Apollo	15
Vocaltones Quartet	16
Wally Fry & Collegians at the Savoy 1955	5
Wally Fry & his Collegians	12
Wally Fry & his Collegians 1955	13
Wally Whyton & Red Sullivan at the Railway	113
Wedgewood Rooms	176
Whiskey River	143
Wrong Direction	132
Young Sue	65
Youth Drifts	70
Youth in Chains	70

INTRODUCTION

I blame Uncle Mac. Like most post-war 'baby boomers' I grew up loving popular music and since my parents preferred more 'serious' stuff it was "Children's Favourites" on Saturday morning BBC radio that got me singing along to pop. In a short time I was sold – an appropriate term since it's cost me a fortune over the past fifty years - but the pleasure has far outweighed that cost.

Next came the teenager-next-door, my cousins and friends' brothers – all that bit older and introducing me to the sounds of Eddie Cochran, Elvis, the Everly Brothers, the Shirelles and (why do I remember this?) John Leyton. Radio Luxembourg helped and from domestic bliss I began sharing musical interests with school friends, before moving into the social world of the pop music at Billy Mannings' "Waltzer" and then the youth club where, unlike school, I met girls.

The mid-60s were the great period of Guildhall concerts, Kimbells, the Rendezvous, the Savoy and most of all the Birdcage hearing some of the greatest live pop ever. I emerged with a familiar dream of fame and fortune, singing and playing around the country in Pompey bands. One of my favourites was Rosemary, who made their debut in Gosport in February 1969, on the bill with a great local band Heaven. We got to know them quite well, including keyboard player Mick Cooper.

Decades later, I had begun researching those great years, with the vague idea of telling the story of our lives as musicians and fans. The archives of the local Evening News in the Library were a major source and I was there one day squinting at the microfilm screen when in walked that same Mick Cooper intent on a similar project. We started talking and sharing our work and from that chance (or was it?) encounter has grown the "Pompey Pop" project. To date, it has included publications, lectures, exhibitions, a blog and our two websites.

This picture book is the latest output from the project, intended to gather together as many images as possible to represent those days, in and around Portsmouth. It is a story, not the story because there are as many stories as there are people who experienced them but we have tried to assemble pictures of the major venues, local acts and events across the broadest range of popular music. "Pompey Pop" is intended to be a catchy, catch-all title but it's about popular music not just Top Twenty 'pop' and includes dance bands, cabaret, folk music, jazz, pop, rock, psychedelia and anything else.

There are some gaps. There's hardly anything here about Pompey's country scene, a couple of good local acts are missing and it would have been nice to have more pictures of audiences and fans. But none of these absences are the result of editorial decisions, it's simply that we asked and didn't get - or couldn't find. There comes a time with a book when you have to go to print but if any of these things emerge in the future they can be added to the websites and the blog.

The book is limited to 1,000 copies with no plan to reprint. Some of the images have been purchased to clear copyright and we know that a few are from notable local photographers like Nigel Grundy, Kevin Purdy, Lawrie Tippins and Terry Aldridge but in many cases we've no idea who took the pictures or how to find out. We'd like to apologise if anyone's offended by the use, but we hope rather that you'll enjoy the celebration of a wonderful period in a great city.

Dave Allen
Summer 2011

In 1956 Rock & Roll came to Britain. In the previous two years there had been the occasional hit for Bill Haley, a cinema 'riot' here and there and an increasing number of dangerous-looking young men walking the streets in drape jackets but it was in 1956 that its impact was felt strongly across the country.

The year began with "Rock Around the Clock" at number one in the British charts and there was a new entry at number 17, Lonnie Donegan's "Rock Island Line" an American song but a style that in the 1950s, grew from the skiffle offshoots of British traditional jazz bands. In the hands of Donegan, Chas McDevitt, the Vipers and others it was a very British sound, and one that many teenagers felt they could emulate. They pinched washboards, broom handles and wooden boxes and *crucially* bought cheap guitars, learned a couple of chords and started playing.

Then in May 1956, Elvis Presley entered the charts for the first time with "Heartbreak Hotel" - and nothing was ever quite the same again. Fats Domino, Carl Perkins, Frankie Lymon, Gene Vincent and others soon followed, captivating a new generation who bought the records, played them on juke boxes in coffee bars, and longed to hear them more often on British radio.

Bill Haley would tour Britain in the spring of 1957 but in the early days, British fans had to be content with glimpses of their heroes at the movies and it was skiffle that often led the way with live performances in coffee bars and youth clubs. Otherwise, popular music in Britain still centred on the bigger dance bands and crooners that had dominated the post-war scene.

Portsmouth was no exception. During the war the South Parade Pier and Savoy Ballrooms had been requisitioned as centres for servicemen – many on their way across the channel on D-Day. In the late 1940s both reverted to entertaining local residents, sailors stationed in Portsmouth and summer holidaymakers from across the country. There was regular work for professional musicians in the theatres and dancehalls and by the mid-fifties there were many active dance bands appearing at the Pier, Savoy and Kimbells ballrooms and other smaller venues.

In October 1953, one of these bands, led by Johnny Lyne, travelled to Manchester and returned as the *Melody Maker's* All-Britain Dance Band Champions. The weekly music paper described the competing bands playing programmes of waltz, quickstep, foxtrot and other formal dances.

That band did not survive long but many of its members, including Johnny, continued to perform locally. Their blind pianist Bill Cole was a much-loved figure around the city for many decades, while drummer Arthur Ward led his own bands in following decades at venues like Clarence Pier and Hayling's Sinah Warren. Other local dance bands led by men like Benny Freedman and Wally Fry were regulars at the seafront ballrooms, often playing support to big names like Ted Heath, Joe Loss, Johnny Dankworth and even Stan Kenton from America.

British musicians took some time to respond to the new sounds of rock & roll but one of the first was jazz drummer Tony Crombie. During the summer of 1956 he formed what is believed to be Britain's first touring and recording rock & roll group, Tony Crombie & his Rockets. On 10 September 1956, they made their live British debut on a variety bill at Portsmouth's Theatre Royal. Portsmouth has few special claims to a place in popular music history but 55 years ago it may have been in at the birth of British Rock & Roll – and it hasn't stopped yet.

PORTSMOUTH HIPPODROME
TELEPHONE 2368

PROGRAMME

| 6.40 | TWICE NIGHTLY COMMENCING MONDAY, MAY 1st, 1939 | 8.50 |

VARIETY

1. OVERTURE ..... *Selected*
2. LES TERRIANOS ..... Tyrolean Acrobatic Novelty
3. AL BURNETT & Company with Marie Rennie ..... In Tit-Bits of 1939
4. REX & BESSIE ..... Australian Dancers
5. G. S. MELVIN ..... Character Comedian
6. AL BURNETT ..... "The Bad Boy from a Good Family"
7. ELIMAR ..... Juggler
8. **INTERMISSION**
   Selection from George Black's Intimate Rag, "BLACK AND BLUE"
   HIPPODROME ORCHESTRA under the direction of JOHN FOWLER
9. LOTTO & CONSTANCE ..... Cycling to Amuse
10. TEX McLEOD ..... Cowboy Humorist
11. First Visit to Portsmouth of the World's Greatest Rhythm Pianist—
    "FATS" WALLER ..... Master of "Swing"
12. AL BURNETT ..... With More Laughs
13. SYLVESTRE ..... The Sunshade Maker

GOD SAVE THE KING

NOTICE
PHOTOGRAPHING IN THEATRE FORBIDDEN
Productions and Variety Acts, being the copyright of the Theatre Proprietors or Variety Artistes, the unauthorised photographing of scenes and acts is illegal.

Fully Licensed Buffet in STALLS and CIRCLE where refreshments at popular prices may be obtained

The Southern Counties Old Time Orchestra 1955

South Parade Pier and Savoy Buildings

Savoy Buildings

Festival of Dance Music 1956 poster

Many professional musicians lived and worked in the city as live music flourished. Wally Fry's band trumpeter Jock Shulman arrived from Glasgow. His daughter became a singer and three of his sons formed Simon Dupree & the Big Sound.

Dancing at the Savoy

Benny Freedman Orchestra outside the Savoy

Wally Fry & Collegians at the Savoy 1955

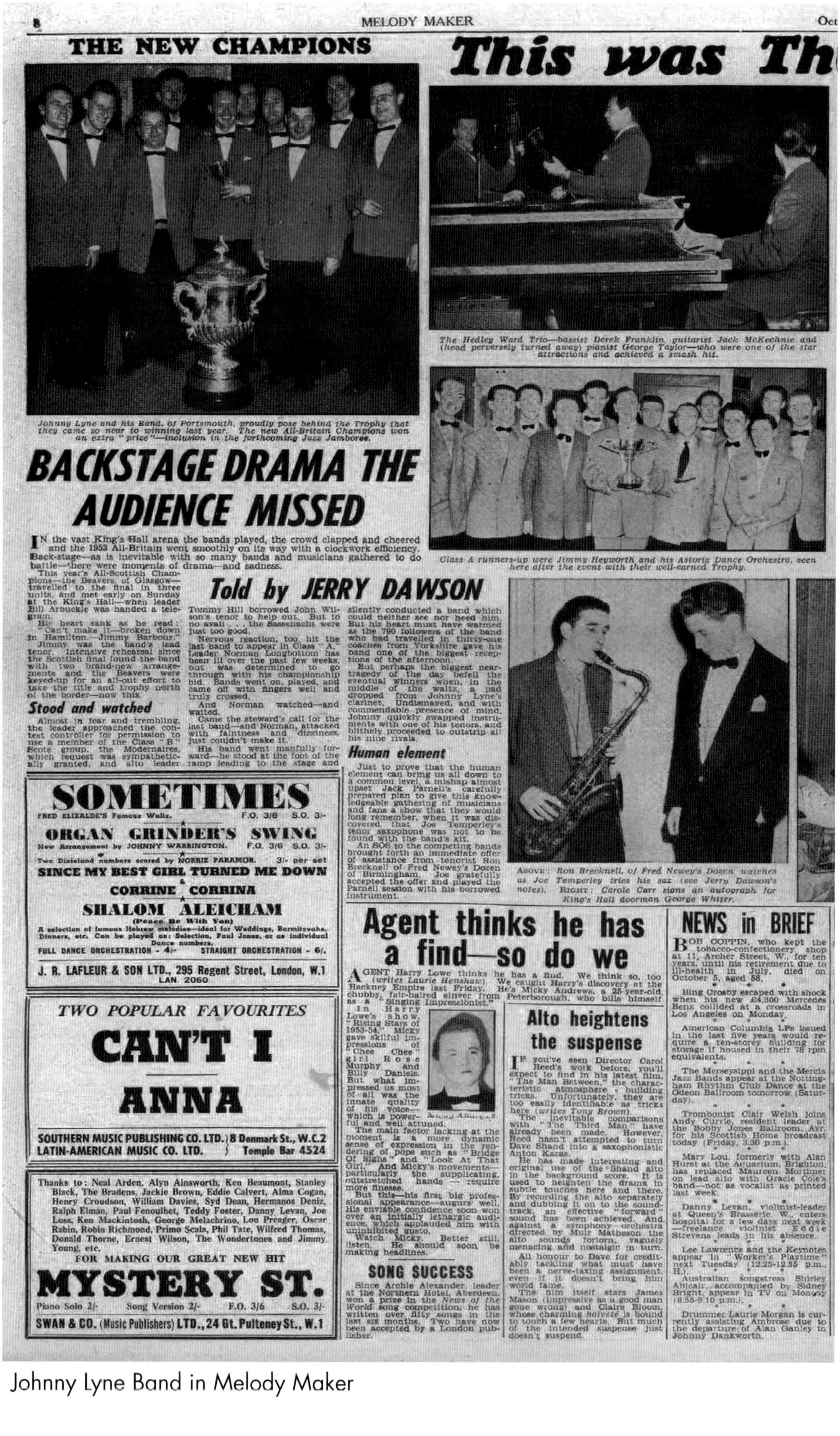

8 MELODY MAKER Oct

THE NEW CHAMPIONS

This was Th

Johnny Lyne and his Band, of Portsmouth, proudly pose behind the Trophy that they came so near to winning last year. The new All-Britain Champions won an extra "prize"—inclusion in the forthcoming Jazz Jamboree.

The Hedley Ward Trio—bassist Derek Franklin, guitarist Jack McKechnie and (head perversely turned away) pianist George Taylor—who were one of the star attractions and achieved a smash hit.

Class A runners-up were Jimmy Heyworth and his Astoria Dance Orchestra, seen here after the event with their well-earned Trophy.

BACKSTAGE DRAMA THE AUDIENCE MISSED

IN the vast King's Hall arena the bands played, the crowd clapped and cheered and the 1953 All-Britain went smoothly on its way with a clockwork efficiency. Back-stage—as is inevitable with so many bands and musicians gathered to do battle—there were moments of drama—and sadness.

Told by JERRY DAWSON

This year's All-Scottish Champions—the Beavers, of Glasgow—travelled to the final in three units, and met early on Sunday at the King's Hall—when leader Bill Arbuckle was handed a telegram.

His heart sank as he read: "Can't make it—broken down in Hamilton.—Jimmy Barbour."

Jimmy was the band's lead tenor. Intensive rehearsal since the Scottish final found the band with two brand-new arrangements and the Beavers were keyed-up for an all-out effort to take the title and trophy north of the border—now this.

Stood and watched

Almost in fear and trembling, the leader approached the contest controller for permission to use a member of the Class "B" Scots group, the Modernaires, which request was sympathetically granted, and alto leader Tommy Hill borrowed John Wilson's tenor to help out. But to no avail . . . the Sassenachs were just too good.

Nervous reaction, too, hit the last band to appear in Class "A." Leader Norman Longbottom has been ill over the past few weeks, but was determined to go through with his championship bid. Bands went on, played, and came off with fingers well and truly crossed.

And Norman watched—and waited.

Came the steward's call for the last band—and Norman, attacked with faintness and dizziness, just couldn't make it.

His band went manfully forward—he stood at the foot of the ramp leading to the stage and silently conducted a band which could neither see nor heed him. But his heart must have warmed as the 790 followers of the band who had travelled in thirty-one coaches from Yorkshire gave his band one of the biggest receptions of the afternoon.

But perhaps the biggest near-tragedy of the day befell the eventual winners when, in the middle of the waltz, a pad dropped from Johnny Lyne's clarinet. Undismayed, and with commendable presence of mind, Johnny quickly swapped instruments with one of his tenors, and blithely proceeded to outstrip all his nine rivals.

Human element

Just to prove that the human element can bring us all down to a common level, a mishap almost upset Jack Parnell's carefully prepared plan to give this knowledgeable gathering of musicians and fans a show that they would long remember, when it was discovered that Joe Temperley's tenor saxophone was not to be found with the band's kit.

An SOS to the competing bands brought forth an immediate offer of assistance from tenorist Ron Brecknell of Fred Newey's Dozen of Birmingham. Joe gratefully accepted the offer and played the Parnell session with his borrowed instrument.

ABOVE: Ron Brecknell, of Fred Newey's Dozen watches as Joe Temperley tries his sax (see Jerry Dawson's notes). RIGHT: Carole Carr signs an autograph for King's Hall doorman George Whiter.

SOMETIMES
FRED ELIZALDE'S Famous Waltz. F.O. 3/6 S.O. 3/-
ORGAN GRINDER'S SWING
New Arrangement by JOHNNY WARRINGTON. F.O. 3/6 S.O. 3/-
Two Dixieland numbers scored by NORRIE PARAMOR. 3/- per set
SINCE MY BEST GIRL TURNED ME DOWN
&
CORRINE CORRINA
SHALOM ALEICHAM
(Peace Be With You)
A selection of famous Hebrew melodies—ideal for Weddings, Barmitzvahs, Dinners, etc. Can be played as: Selection, Paul Jones, or as individual Dance numbers.
FULL DANCE ORCHESTRATION - 4/- STRAIGHT ORCHESTRATION - 6/.
J. R. LAFLEUR & SON LTD., 295 Regent Street, London, W.1
LAN. 2060

TWO POPULAR FAVOURITES
CAN'T I
ANNA
SOUTHERN MUSIC PUBLISHING CO. LTD. } 8 Denmark St., W.C.2
LATIN-AMERICAN MUSIC CO. LTD. } Temple Bar 4524

Thanks to: Neal Arden, Alyn Ainsworth, Ken Beaumont, Stanley Black, The Bradens, Jackie Brown, Eddie Calvert, Alma Cogan, Henry Croudson, William Davies, Syd Dean, Hermanos Deniz, Ralph Elman, Paul Fenoulhet, Teddy Foster, Danny Levan, Joe Loss, Ken Mackintosh, George Melachrino, Lou Preager, Oscar Rabin, Robin Richmond, Primo Scala, Phil Tate, Wilfred Thomas, Donald Thorne, Ernest Wilson, The Wondertones and Jimmy Young, etc.
FOR MAKING OUR GREAT NEW HIT
MYSTERY ST.
Piano Solo 2/- Song Version 2/- F.O. 3/6 S.O. 3/-
SWAN & CO. (Music Publishers) LTD., 24 Gt. Pulteney St., W.1

Agent thinks he has a find—so do we

AGENT Harry Lowe thinks he has a find. We think so, too (writes Laurie Henshaw). We caught Harry's discovery at the Hackney Empire last Friday. He's Micky Andrews, a 25-year-old, chubby, fair-haired singer from Peterborough, who bills himself as a "Singing Impressionist."

In Harry Lowe's show, "Rising Stars of 1953-54," Micky gave skilful impressions of "Chee Chee" girl Rose Murphy and Billy Daniels. But what impressed us most of all was the innate quality of his voice—which is powerful and well attuned.

Micky Andrews

The main factor lacking at the moment is a more dynamic sense of expression in the rendering of pops such as "Bridge Of Sighs" and "Look At That Girl." And Micky's movements—particularly the supplicating, outstretched hands — require more finesse.

But this—his first big professional appearance—augurs well. His enviable confidence soon won over an initially lethargic audience, which applauded him with uninhibited gusto.

Watch Micky. Better still, listen. He should soon be making headlines.

SONG SUCCESS

Since Archie Alexander, leader at the Northern Hotel, Aberdeen, won a prize in the *News of the World* song competition, he has written over fifty songs in the last six months. Two have now been accepted by a London publisher.

Alto heightens the suspense

IF you've seen Director Carol Reed's work before, you'll expect to find in his latest film, "The Man Between," the characteristic atmosphere - building tricks. Unfortunately, they are too easily identifiable as tricks here (*writes Tony Brown*).

The inevitable comparisons with "The Third Man" have already been made. However, Reed hasn't attempted to turn Dave Shand into a saxophonistic Anton Karas.

He has made interesting and original use of the Shand alto in the background score. It is used to heighten the drama in subtle touches here and there. By recording the alto separately and dubbing it on to the soundtrack, an effective "forward" sound has been achieved. And against a symphony orchestra directed by Muir Matheson the alto sounds forlorn, vaguely menacing and nostalgic in turn.

All honour to Dave for creditably tackling what must have been a nerve-taxing assignment, even if it doesn't bring him world fame.

The film itself stars James Mason (impressive as a good man gone wrong) and Claire Bloom, whose charming *naivete* is bound to touch a few hearts. But much of the intended suspense just doesn't suspend.

NEWS in BRIEF

BOB COPPIN, who kept the tobacco-confectionery shop at 11, Archer Street, W., for ten years, until his retirement due to ill-health in July, died on October 5, aged 58.

Bing Crosby escaped with shock when his new £4,300 Mercedes Benz collided at a crossroads in Los Angeles on Monday.

American Columbia LPs issued in the last five years would require a ten-storey building for storage if housed in their 78 rpm equivalents.

The Merseysippi and the Mercia Jazz Bands appear at the Nottingham Rhythm Club Dance at the Odeon Ballroom tomorrow (Saturday).

Trombonist Clair Welsh joins Andy Currie, resident leader at the Bobby Jones Ballroom, Ayr, for his Scottish Home broadcast today (Friday, 3.30 p.m.).

Mary Lou, formerly with Alan Hurst at the Aquarium, Brighton, has replaced Maureen Mortimer on lead alto with Gracie Cole's band—not as vocalist as printed last week.

Danny Levan, violinist-leader at Queen's Brasserie, W., enters hospital for a few days next week—freelance violinist Eddie Strevens leads in his absence.

Lee Lawrence and the Keynotes appear in "Worker's Playtime" next Tuesday (12.25-12.55 p.m., H.).

Australian songstress Shirley Abicair, accompanied by Sidney Bright, appear in TV on Monday (8.55-9.10 p.m.).

Drummer Laurie Morgan is currently assisting Ambrose due to the departure of Alan Ganley to Johnny Dankworth.

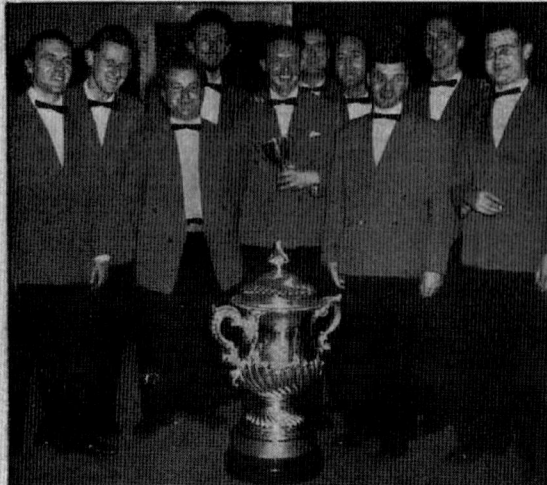

Johnny Lyne Band in Melody Maker

October 17, 1953 MELODY MAKER 9

The Red-Letter Day of the Semi-Pro Bands

THE MELODY MAKER annual All-Britain Dance Band Championship should be a deadly-dull affair. Consider this: Last Sunday we had 15 part-time bands who appeared in turn, in varying degrees of nervousness, each to play a set programme of one foxtrot, one waltz, one quickstep.

No band was bound to play its programme in that order and, in fact, there were contradictory opinions as to the advisability of opening with the waltz, quickstep or foxtrot.

No matter. We heard a succession of bands play a succession of these. It went on for about three hours. How could it be bearable, let alone entertaining?

Yet it is this show that year after year fills the huge King's Hall in Manchester's Belle Vue.

There is no other show so apparently lacking in variety, yet, paradoxically, the All-Britain is a unique entertainment in the world of dance music.

Of course, there were first-class professional entertainers on the bill. There was the kind of performance from the Hedley Ward Trio that would stop any normal Variety bill.

The audience loved them.

By then, it had sat judiciously through the appearance of five Class B bands. The best of these—the Modernaires, from Muirkirk, Scotland—played above their grading, and might have sat in with the section A men undetected, had not some of the boys tended toward sharpness upstairs and overblowing.

It wouldn't be fair to run too rigorous a musical rule over these relatively inexperienced contestants. Class B is to be regarded as the nursery of the Contests scheme. Such men limit their ambition laudably to improving sufficiently for Class A grading the following season.

TONY BROWN DESCRIBES THE 1953 ALL-BRITAIN

But there were promising musicians to be heard; there were potentially good bands. We heard a very creditably handled soprano sax from the tenor player with the Meloman Quintet, an East London group. And its guitarist played some fast passages fluently and proved himself a sound all-round performer.

In the name of justice, the Woodchoppers from Farnworth must be mentioned. They opened the show. This is a difficult enough spot for the veteran. For the comparative novice, it is murder. Any band can fall to pieces with nerves. All honour to this Lancashire group that it didn't. Its biggest deficiency is its inexperience. That is the easiest of all handicaps to overcome.

The first Class A participants to show themselves were Scotland's pride — the Beavers, from Glasgow. They were placed third last year. They are Kenton admirers, and as such gave a lusty performance. We heard some careless intonation in a trombone solo during the foxtrot. We admired the vigour and enthusiasm of the band; we would have appreciated some subtlety, too.

In the waltz there was an unhappily scored passage for trombone against four clarinets and baritone, and one trombone was noticeably sharp in the ensemble. On the whole, the band did not match its showing of last year.

Well-nigh perfect

Next on was a Palais band. It played beautifully as a Palais band. In fact, the Jimmy Heyworth Dance Orchestra must be well nigh perfect for dancing. It played steadily, had a beautifully fat, smooth ensemble sound. But it had the limitations of its style—arrangements too simple to exploit to the full the capabilities of the musicians. The quickstep was bouncy rather than beaty. And the lead alto was outblown by the rest of the section throughout.

An unusual but pointless intro led the next band, the Fred Newey Dozen, into its quickstep, making the first chorus an anti-climax. The intricate alto and tenor unison passage was well executed. But there was some uncertainty from one of the trumpets here and there. The saxes were smooth in a stolid waltz and maintained the standard in the foxtrot. But the trumpet section deteriorated in this last number, with the lead overblowing and a more noticeable uncertainty in the opening bars. A precise, well-rehearsed but uninspired performance.

Favourites

Johnny Lyne's Portsmouth crew were probably favourites for a win. They were second last year, when Johnny made his mark as about the most impressive figure in Contests. In the band, one can trace something of a Sauter-Finegan influence. The arrangements are intricate, modern, ambitious. But they are played by men who understand what they are doing.

If the band has a fault, it is the fault of that dominating personality, Johnny Lyne, who expresses one facet of his skill in complicated scoring. There is something happening every few bars; there are changes of tone colour as often; there are counter-melodies; there are intriguing instrumental combinations.

In the foxtrot, for example, there were two clarinets, trumpet and trombone against an interplay of figures between the baritone and tenor—all backed by a quietly riding rhythm.

And there was Johnny himself fronting the band, playing a few bars on trumpet and making hasty swops to alto and clarinet. He plays the alto very well in the fashionable cool manner, and clarinet and trumpet very competently.

Cool, relaxed

He is quite some leader; he has quite some orchestra. Without Johnny, the band might not stand out in a crowd. It has his arranging strength, possibly his immaturity, too. It is an interesting band in an academic way. It is not at the moment as exciting as it might be.

It needs a high standard of musicianship to play in the style of the Top Five. It is cool and relaxed, never startling. Such music can only be remarkable for its performance. The two front-line men played smoothly, whether in harmony, unison or solo. It was restrained; it was musicianly. It wasn't dynamic.

This Home Counties outfit was followed by a group of similar policy. The Wolverhampton Quintet were tasteful as always and played with the beautiful understanding they displayed to win the championship last year. There was Jack Clarke's wonderfully controlled sub-tone tenor, drummer Billau's dexterous brush work, the sensitive accordion of Woodhouse—but it is invidious to select names. All the boys play so well together. Unfortunately they stuck to the melody in nearly everything. It was practically faultless, but not the stuff we expect from All-Britain champions.

Best saxes

Best sax section in the whole event was that led by trumpeter Brian Jenner. Where they scored over all others was in the matching of tones. They achieved a round, complete, cohesive sound. A pity there is no award for sections. This ensemble was well led by Jenner, in spite of his over-wide vibrato.

London's Fred Anderson did not take the stand with his band. Perhaps he was thus able to judge it dispassionately. It has a very high potential—a lot higher than the arrangements it plays. There were some praiseworthy moments: very smooth sub-tone unison in the foxtrot, a good soprano-led sax section in the last chorus; a pleasantly discordant coda to the quickstep.

There was overdone tuned tom-tom rhythm in Raymond Kaye's foxtrot which didn't always suit the harmonic demands of the tune. But it was a very good arrangement. The wild excitement of the intro to "Idaho" was right out of keeping with the number. And the trumpets were sharp.

Norman Longbottom and his Music closed the proceedings—and aptly. It is a stylish band. We heard very nice phrasing from the alto soloist in the first number and very smooth unison from the saxes in one beautifully scored passage.

The trumpets did not come up to this standard, and that became increasingly apparent toward the end. And the band finished with an ordinary sort of arrangement. The arrangements as a whole were pedestrian.

There was the contest, then. So close were several of the bands that many of the loudly canvassed predictions of my neighbours might have been implemented by the judges. But really, it was obvious that this was Johnny Lyne's day. No band played better, no band had so much to play. And Johnny was the Musician Of The Day in every sense. He worthily carried off the championship and award. I wouldn't quarrel with the verdict at all.

It was unfortunate that one section of the crowd was so impatient to hear the Jack Parnell Band. This gave Carole Carr an undeservedly rough passage. She sang well and looked beautiful. And she handled ill-mannered tantrums with rare good humour.

Nevertheless, the crowd was yelling for Parnell. When it got Parnell, it yelled for "The Champ." I suppose that's a compliment. Eventually he played it and tore the house down.

But not before we'd heard beautiful solos from Bob Burns, Lad Busby and Jo Hunter. And not before we'd listened enthralled (most of us) to Jimmy Watson's wonderful "April In Paris" score.

For me, that was the finest climax to an amazingly musical afternoon.

BBC disc-jockey Wilfrid Thomas in typical stance as he compered the entire event.

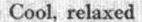

Dennis Hale snapped during the Parnell session.

RESULTS

CHAMPIONSHIP SECTION "A"

Winners: JOHNNY LYNE ORCHESTRA (171 marks) (3 tenors, baritone, trombone, trumpet, piano, bass, drums, bongoes). All coms.: J. Lyne, 273, Arundel Street, Portsmouth.

Second: JIMMY HEYWORTH AND HIS ASTORIA DANCE ORCHESTRA (165 marks) (2 tenors, 2 altos, baritone, 3 trumpets, 2 trombones, piano, bass, drums). All coms.: J. Heyworth, 1, Caernarvon Avenue, Burnley, Lancs.

Third: FRED ANDERSON'S "CABARET" DANCE BAND (157 marks) (2 altos, 2 tenors, baritone, trumpet, piano, bass, drums). All coms.: F. Anderson, 22, Hermit Road, E.16.

Outstanding Musician: Johnny Lyne (trumpet, alto, clarinet, soprano), Johnny Lyne Orchestra.

CHAMPIONSHIP SECTION "B"

First: THE MODERNAIRES (alto, 2 tenors, baritone, trumpet, piano, bass, drums). All coms.: T. Hill, 4, Furnace Road, Muirkirk, Ayrshire.

Second: THE WOODCHOPPERS DANCE ORCHESTRA (3 trumpets, 2 altos, 2 tenors, piano, bass, drums). All coms.: Harold Jobbins, 1, Norfolk Street, Farnworth, Lancs.

THE CLASS B WINNERS

Thomas Hill, leader of the Modernaires, receives the Class B winners' Trophy from Pat Brand.

Class B runners-up were the Woodchoppers Dance Orchestra, whose leader, Harold Jobbins, receives the Trophy.

FEATURE SPOT!

Clavioline at the RADIO SHOW

"Clavioline" on a P.C. will bring details of the PROFESSIONAL Keyboard.

Selmer

114-116 CHARING CROSS ROAD LONDON, W.C.2. TEM. 0444

MUSICAL high-spot of the Radio Show was the succession of Clavioline interludes.

Once again, this PROFESSIONAL Keyboard made history—chosen to represent MUSIC in the big ELECTRONIC show. You are well advised to follow the lead of the broadcasting and electronic experts, and choose the Clavioline as your stairway to success.

OLD TIME and SEQUENCE DANCES

Berlins Waltz Cotillon
Boston Two Step
Carnival Square Dance
Choristers' Waltz
Davidson's Paul Jones
Davidson's Saunter
Davidson's Waltzes
Dream Saunter
Dutch Foursome
Early Doors Quadrilles
Eightsome Reel
Esperano Barn Dance
Eton Boating Song
Evergreen Quadrilles
Festival Of Britain Waltz
Floradora Lancers
Fylde Waltz
Gainsborough Glide
Hearts Of Oak Lancers
Heather Bells (Latchford Schottische)
Her Golden Hair Barn Dance
Hurndilla
Imperial Waltz
Inspiration Veleta
Joyous Moments (La Rinka)
Kings Waltz
Latchford Schottische
Lauder Quadrilles
La Varsovianna
Lilac Waltz
Lola Tango
Marie Mazurka
Maxina
Poor John Barn Dance
Prince Charming (Waltz Cotillon)
Regimental Daughters (Marine 4-Step)
Saunter Serenade
Savoy Schottische
Seaside Saunter
Skirl O' the Pipes
Songe D'Automne (Waltz)
South Bank Shuffle
Stroll Along Saunter
Take Your Partners (Waltz Cotillon)
Thompson's Barn Dance Medley No. 1
Thompson's Barn Dance Medley No. 2
Thompson's Barn Dance Medley No. 3
Thompson's March Medley
Thompson's Waltz Medley
Tell Me You Love Me
Truro Gavotte
Underneath the Stars Saunter
Valse Superbe
Veleta
Victoria Cross (Mil. Two Step)
Vision of Salome (Waltz)
Waltz for the Queen
Waltz of Britain
White Heather Caledonians
Yearning Saunter

PRICE: Orchestrations 3/6d. each. Extra P.c's 1/- each. Violin parts 6d. each.

FRANCIS, DAY & HUNTER, LTD.
138-140 CHARING CROSS ROAD, LONDON, W.C.2
TEMple Bar 9351

Johnny Lyne Band in Melody Maker

Arthur Ward Band with pianist Bill Cole

Johnny Lyne Band

Lyne's rhythm section

The Reginald Bannistra band at the Empress Ballroom 1957/8

Alf Hallman & his Orchestra 1956

Arthur Ward Band at Clarence Pier 1960s

Reginald Bannistra & his Music 1955

Graham Leslie & his Orchestra 1956

The Dance Orchestra of HM Royal Marines 1955

The Combined Theatres Orchestra 1955

Wally Fry & his Collegians

Wally Fry & his Collegians 1955

Benny Freedman Orchestra

Ron Bennett & the Club Quintet 1955

The Chiz Bishop Quartet 1956

George Turner manager of the Savoy at the cricket

South Parade Pier Summer Programme

EVERY WEDNESDAY AFTERNOON
(July 3rd to September 4th) at 4 p.m.
we present
GLAMOUR AND GRACIOUSNESS AT GRAND
BATHING BEAUTY CONTESTS
Heats to find "MISS SOUTHSEA OF 1957"
(Finals—September 4th)
Sponsored by the DAILY SKETCH
£150 Prize Money distributed through Heats and Final
GIRLS! Bring Your Favourite Costume and win your
Holiday Expenses!
A NATIONAL PAPER may help you to become a NATIONAL STAR
Entry Forms on application

CRUISING through the BLUE WATERS of the SOLENT

Delightful Steamer Excursions

DAILY FROM THE PIER HEAD, FROM WHITSUN
To ISLE OF WIGHT including direct excursion to RYDE, SANDOWN,
SHANKLIN, VENTNOR. Also to BOURNEMOUTH & SOUTHAMPTON DOCKS to view the "QUEENS" and other Great Liners.
SHORT TRIPS HOURLY ROUND PORTSMOUTH HARBOUR, ETC.

FOR THE YOUNG AND THE YOUNG IN HEART
GRAND AMUSEMENT ARCADE
with all the Latest Novelties and Machines

LARGE WELL-APPOINTED
LICENSED BARS
OVER THE SEA!
A FREE HOUSE SERVING THE DRINKS OF YOUR CHOICE
in
"THE BAR ON THE BRINY"

DANCING
In the BALLROOM
Nightly (Monday to Saturday) 8-11 p.m., to
WALLY FRY and his COLLEGIANS
In the OPEN AIR—DECK BANDSTAND
Mondays, Wednesdays, Saturdays, 9-10.30, to
BEN OAKLEY and his ORCHESTRA

PORTSMOUTH CORPORATION
SOUTH PARADE PIER
SOUTHSEA

Entertainments Manager (for Portsmouth Corporation):
DAVID EVANS, F.I.M.E.M.

Box Office - 10 a.m.—8 p.m.
Telephone - - - 32289 (2 lines)

WED. 26th JUNE at 7.45 THURS. 27th JUNE to SAT. 14th SEPT.—
TWICE NIGHTLY at 6.0 & 8.20

JACK HYLTON and CHESNEY ALLEN present
Southsea's Great Resident Summer Show

"JUMP FOR JOY."

Starring

REG DIXON

The famous Star of Stage, Radio and Television

with

SALLY BARNES ★ **ERNEST ARNLEY and GLORIA DAY**

and Great West End Cast

TWO SEPARATE PROGRAMMES   CHANGING ON THURSDAY
Reserved : Stalls 6/- & 4/6 ; Circle 5/- ; Sides 3/6
Children half price First House

Just a few more reasons why you must make it
SOUTHSEA for your HOLIDAYS

The Vocaltones & talent scout Carroll Levis at the Apollo Cinema, Albert Road

The Vocaltones Quartet

The Liddell Sisters mime act

The Gary Hayman Trio

Signed for the Liddells - Dickie Valentine

> The Liddell Sisters became the Honeys. Over the next decade they appeared on bills with Cliff Richard, the Beatles, Helen Shapiro, Englebert Humperdinck, Ken Dodd, Tommy Steele, Adam Faith, Larry Grayson and others

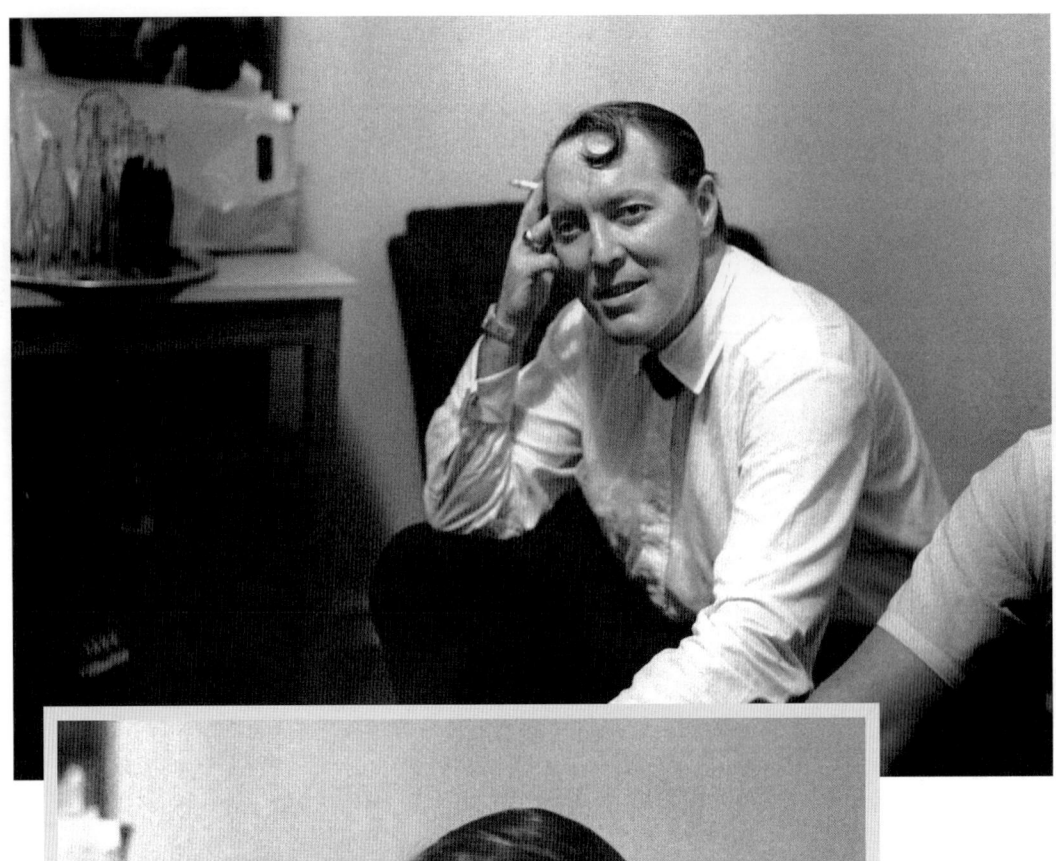

Bill Haley at Portsmouth Guildhall

Pompey Pop 19

Theatre Royal

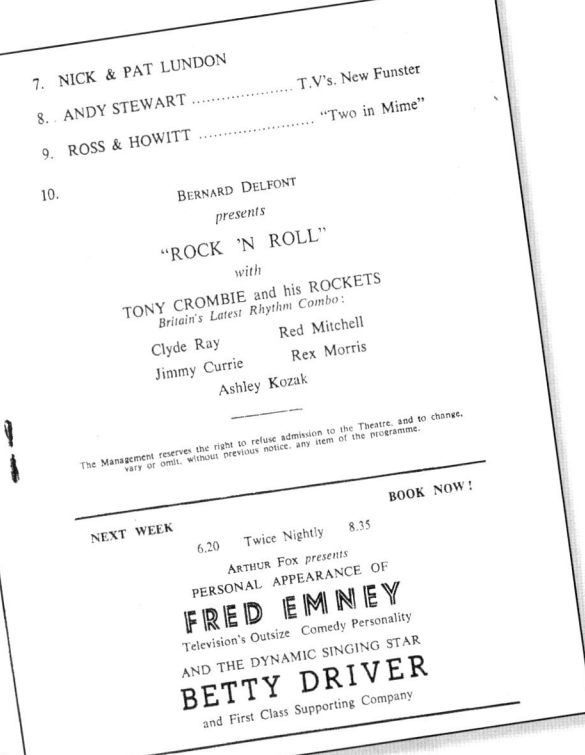
Theatre Royal Programme Sept 1956

"ROCK 'N' ROLL" GREETED WITH CHEERS

SCREAMS, stamping feet, and the incessant clap, clap of a feverish, shirt-sleeved sweatered teenage audience launched "Rock 'n' Roll" on to the British variety stage at the Theatre Royal, Portsmouth, last night.

This was no wild, riotous debut for "Rock 'n' Roll"—the most controversial music craze since the Charleston — but one which ended with cheering and applause that rocked the theatre.

Call it mass hysteria, exhibitionism or plain audience participation. The title matters not at all. "Rock 'n' Roll" may die soon, but at the moment it is a lusty, rowdy, healthy infant.

The man who recognizes this is drummer Tony Crombie, who has faith enough in it to lay out £400 to form the new group.

It was he and the five other members of the "combo" who caused all the excitement last night.

From the start, he had them clapping to the infectious rhythm, and like wildfire, it spread from the youthful element in the upper circle to the older folk below; yes, to two members of the orchestra.

Faults? Basically, the tenor saxophone sufficiently dominant exactly the sound achieved on recordings. one liked it all the same.

But this show is fa wholly "Rock 'n' Roll" Coloured singer Daniels has a charm good voice that will out craze.

Humour has its pla Andy Stewart, who co the show, and Johnny are talented young co while pianist Billy Wy singer Don Fox add musical side.

Clever mimers Ros Howitt, and dancers N Pat Lundon, complete

Rock & Roll review Sept 1956

American singer Johnny Preston (left) with bandleader Tony Crombie, 1960 (Photo by Popperfoto/Getty Images)

The Hi Fis

Tony & Gill in Paulsgrove

John Pounds Youth Club

Bert Parker & Peter Hicks

DP as 'Tommy Steele'

Geoff, Spliff, DP

South Parade Pier 1950s

Getting ready at the Railway

Railway Hotel

Acker Bilk at the Savoy 1960

Barry McCarthy & his Dixielanders 1955

Barry McCarthy & his Dixielanders 1956

Vieux Carre Jazzband at the Rendezvous Club 1960

Kid Martyn Band at the Rendezvous

The Saints skiffle group at Somerstown Youth Club

The Thunderclaps

The Tea Chest bass

The Saints

ROCK 'N' ROLL, 1958
Become a member now of Portsmouth's
Leading Jive Club!
RICKY'S CLUB
Goldsmith Ave. Tel. 341611
WED., FRI., SAT., SUN. 8 - 11.30   THURS. 8 - 11
FULL BUFFET FACILITIES

THE GUILDHALL
PORTSMOUTH

BUD FREEMAN
with
ALEX WELSH
AND HIS BAND
TUESDAY, OCT. 11th at 7.30 p.m.

STALLS
3/6
TO BE RETAINED

TICKETS CANNOT BE EXCHANGED OR MONEY REFUNDED
FOR ENTRANCE AND CAR PARKS SEE PLAN ON BACK
Acme Printing Co. Ltd, Portsmouth

E
ADMIT AT
NORTH
EAST
DOOR

ROW
R
SEAT
44

The Thunderclaps

Demons skiffle group

Dancing at Ricky's Club

Ricky's Club Goldsmith Avenue

Jamming at Ricky's

Inaugural Jazz Concert

in the

New Guildhall, Tuesday, 9th June, 1959

by

Chris Barber's Jazz Band

Personnel—Chris Barber (*trombone*), Monty Sunshine (*clarinet*), Pat Halcox (*trumpet*), Eddie Smith (*banjo*), Dick Smith (*bass*), Graham Burbidge (*drums*), Ottilie Patterson (*vocals*).

Items to be selected from—

Bourbon Street Parade	When Things Go Wrong
Sheik of Araby	Trombone Charlie
Black and Tan Fantasy	Strange Things Are Happening
Lawd, You've Sure Been Good to Me	Every Day
	Mama Don't Allow
Eh La Bas	New Blues
You Took advantage of Me	Willy The Weeper
Sweet Sue	Mean Mistreater
Beale Street Blues	Yama Yama Man
Too Many Drivers	Old Man Mose
Stop Now It's Praying Time	Mood Indigo
Majorca	Bear Cat Crawl
Tiger Rag	Lowland Blues
Saturday Night Function	Panama
Old Rugged Cross	Savoy Blues
Hushabie	Lonesome Road
When You and I Were Young Maggie	Bill Bailey
	Moonshine Man
Indiana	You Rascal You

GOD SAVE THE QUEEN

There will be an Interval at approx. 9 p

There are Licensed Bars in the Circle Foyer and Lower also Service for Coffees and Light Refreshme

Chris Barber Guildhall Programme

CHRIS BARBER LAUNCHED JAZZ AT THE GUILDHALL, BOMBED IN 1941 AND RE-OPENED BY HM THE QUEEN 18 YEARS LATER

LONDONER NAT GONELLA, STAR OF THE PRE-WAR JAZZ AND DANCE BANDS, SPENT HIS LATER LIFE IN GOSPORT, OFTEN APPEARING AT LOCAL JAZZ EVENTS

Nat Gonella tribute in Gosport

As the 1950s drew to a close, Britain produced its first rock & roll stars, Tommy Steele and Cliff Richard and teenagers around Portsmouth began amplifying guitars and swapping washboards for basic drum kits. So it was that members of the Saints Skiffle Group became the Cadillacs and, complete with red drape suits, played the latest rock & roll hits – often starting out in schools and youth clubs. Elsewhere schoolmates formed groups like the Renegades (from the Building School) or the Residents (Copnor Secondary Modern).

But the dance bands survived albeit with greater competition and a less certain future. Some of these accomplished musicians also took the opportunity to explore newer sounds in modern jazz and there was a growing local traditional jazz scene – not least in clubs like the "Rendezvous" which began in an old church in Ashburton Road, Southsea and pubs like the Cobden Arms in Arundel Street or the Railway Hotel, behind Fratton Station. There were also top touring acts at the Savoy and South Parade Pier.

Portsmouth's Guildhall opened in 1890 but 51 years later, German bombers destroyed it and the Hippodrome Theatre opposite which, a few months before the war, had featured a week with Fats Waller. The Hippodrome never returned but in June 1959 HM the Queen opened the rebuilt Guildhall and it soon became a venue for most of the top acts of the period. One of the first acts to appear was Chris Barber's Jazz Band and those who followed included Louis Armstrong, BB King, the Beatles, Ray Charles, Miles Davis, Duke Ellington, Ella Fitzgerald, Jimi Hendrix, Modern Jazz Quartet, the Motown Revue, Muddy Waters, Pink Floyd, Cliff Richard & the Shadows, the Rolling Stones, Nina Simone and Sarah Vaughan.

One of the most popular smaller venues of the period was Ricky's Club in Goldsmith Avenue opposite the footbridge to the station. Here teenagers could dance to records or local rock & roll groups while visiting musicians enjoyed the opportunity of after-hours jam sessions. Larger halls like the Oddfellows (Kingston Road) and cinemas like the Troxy (Fratton Road) promoted new pop stars including Cliff Richard & the Shadows, Billy Fury and Adam Faith and the Savoy Ballroom began booking the new guitar-based acts as well as the dance bands.

Portsmouth produced its first 'rocking' stars. The Mick Glover Group were very popular around 1958 and while Mick was on National Service in the RAF they were renamed the Live Five and appeared briefly in Expresso Bongo. Vocal trios the Freemen and the Honeys both worked nationally and internationally – often with major stars, and Portsmouth produced its first real recording artist, Frank Kelly who with the Hunters released a number of singles and was featured regularly on package tours.

Many skiffle players moved to rock & roll but the roots of that music in American folk and blues and the popularity of acoustic guitars contributed to the early years of the folk revival which would be in full swing around Portsmouth by the mid-1960s.

The first coffee bars now had juke-boxes, the youth clubs were beginning to respond to current pop hits and even the BBC (and newer ITV) did their best with pop shows like "Oh Boy" and "Six Five Special". But on the radio it was Luxembourg rather than the Light Programme that provided most interest – especially when the first transistor radios appeared in 1960.

The Denver Four

The Hot Rods

Pompey Pop   33

The Mustangs

The Hot Rods

Brothers Scarlett start out

Pete White

Tremors

Tremors

Cadillacs

Cadillacs

Cadillacs 1957

Cadillacs at Court School of Dancing

Cadillacs NY Eve '59 Hillside Youth Club

> MIKE GLOVER'S DREAMS OF STARDOM WERE DISRUPTED BY NATIONAL SERVICE BUT THOSE REMAINING RE-FORMED AS THE LIVE FIVE, APPEARING BRIEFLY IN THE MOVIE EXPRESSO BONGO WITH CLIFF RICHARD. MIKE GLOVER LIVES IN NORTH HAMPSHIRE AND STILL PERFORMS

Mick & Mrs Glover - Gill Hutchins (Crestas)

Mick Glover Group

Live Five in the movie *Expresso Bongo*

The Honeys & Cliff

The Honeys

EVENING NEWS, SATURDAY, NOVEMBER 2, 1957

"Rock 'n' Roll" Group to Appear on TV

FIVE young Portsmouth musicians may be on the theshold of fame.

They have been promised a television appearance for winning the final heat in the second house of the Carroll Levis discovery show, which was recently at Southsea.

The agent who found Tommy Steele thinks that the group, the Mike Glover Rock 'n' Rollers, has a chance of film work.

Leader of the group is 19-year-old apprentice chef, Mike Glover, of 27, Algiers Road, Copnor, who plays an electric guitar.

Playing the other electric guitar is Barry Barron (19), of 85, Goldsmith Avenue, Fratton. He works in the second-hand car business with his father.

Bass player is Dave Barber (16), an apprentice welder, of 54, Somers Road North, Fratton.

Mike Orton (18), of 108, Tangier Road, Copnor, who scrabbles the washboard, is a plumber's apprentice with the City Engineering Department.

The drummer is 17-year-old Terry Wiseman, of 55, Kimbolton Road, Copnor.

The group has won the title of champions of the South Coast.

Headline News

GIORA GODIK

PRESENTS

CLIFF RICHARD
THE SHADOWS

Daily and Wayne

The Honeys

Bill Finch

●

Public Relations, Press and Publicity — **Arie Gelblum**
In Association with **S. Shai**
Advertising Agency **D. Belkin**
Programme — **Alpern—Melamed**

Israel, September—October 1963

Cliff & Honeys on tour

The Honeys

The Honeys & Bobby Vee

The Honeys & Adam Faith

The Freemen

Dancing at Ricky's

Jazz at the Railway Hotel

Clarence Pier Ballroom

44 Pompey Pop

The Guildhall Square

THE GUILDHALL SQUARE WAS NOT YET A PEDESTRIAN PRECINCT BUT A BUSY THOROUGHFARE FOR CARS AND BUSES. THERE WERE A NUMBER OF PUBS IN THE VICINITY OFFERING LIVE MUSIC, VERRECHIA'S CAFÉ AND THE ANNUAL STUDENTS' 'STWEEKOTHEQUE'.

The Guildhall opens 1959

Guildhall now

Pompey Pop   45

Southern Sounds at the Guildhall

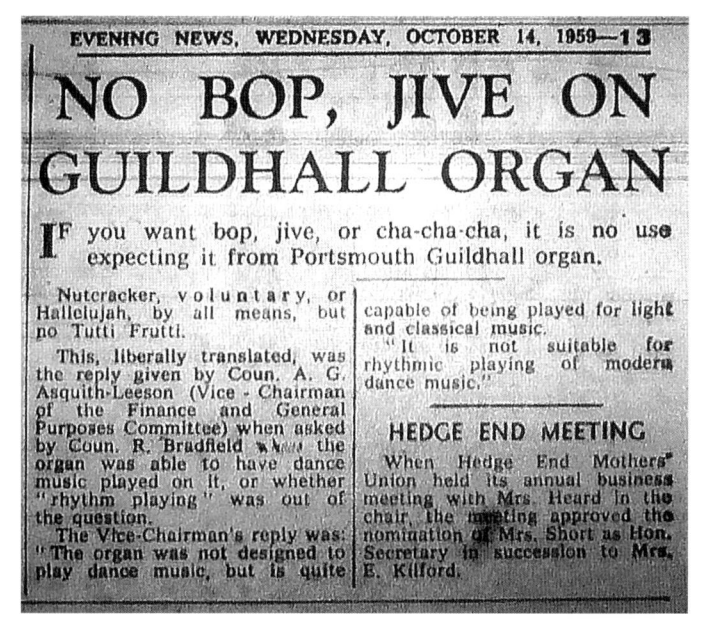

EVENING NEWS, WEDNESDAY, OCTOBER 14, 1959—13

NO BOP, JIVE ON GUILDHALL ORGAN

IF you want bop, jive, or cha-cha-cha, it is no use expecting it from Portsmouth Guildhall organ.

Nutcracker, voluntary, or Hallelujah, by all means, but no Tutti Frutti.

This, liberally translated, was the reply given by Coun. A. G. Asquith-Leeson (Vice-Chairman of the Finance and General Purposes Committee) when asked by Coun. R. Bradfield whether the organ was able to have dance music played on it, or whether "rhythm playing" was out of the question.

The Vice-Chairman's reply was: "The organ was not designed to play dance music, but is quite capable of being played for light and classical music.

"It is not suitable for rhythmic playing of modern dance music."

HEDGE END MEETING

When Hedge End Mothers' Union held its annual business meeting with Mrs. Heard in the chair, the meeting approved the nomination of Mrs. Short as Hon. Secretary in succession to Mrs. E. Kilford.

Guildhall organ

Cobden Arms, with the Guildhall in the distance

Tony Porter

Frank Kelly & the Crestas

The Crestas

Frank Kelly & Hunters

FRANK KELLY with the *Hunters* 'Send me the Pillow'

Frank Kelly

Frank Kelly & the Hunters at the Royal Southampton 1959

Frank Kelly in the mid '60s

SEND ME THE PILLOW
(THAT YOU DREAM ON)
RECORDED BY
JOHNNY TILLOTSON
ON LONDON
RUSS SAINTY
ON H.M.V.
MARTY WILDE
ON PHILIPS
FRANK KELLY
ON FONTANA
FOUR STAR SALES PUB. INC U.S.A.
BENS MUSIC LTD LONDON
Sole Selling Agents
Kassner Associated Publishers Ltd.
Kassner House, 25, Denmark St. LONDON. W.C.2.
2/6

FULL CHART-POINT RESULTS FOR 1962
127 STAR RATINGS
HOTEL HAPPINESS
SOUL BOSSA NOVA
new MUSICAL EXPRESS
JOHNNY TILLOTSON
Hot Smash Hit!
FRANK KELLY
THE HUNTERS
I SAW LINDA YESTERDAY
267 261 TF
Fontana
THE SMASH!!
LOO-BE-LOO
THE CHUCKS on DECCA F 11569
"THE TWIST"!
THIS IS BIGGER!!

THE
HUNTERS

WILSON AGENCY
LONDON
LAN. 9841

Frank Kelly mid '60s

Frank Kelly & the Digger Hart Combo

Pompey Pop 51

For-Tunes

For-Tunes

For-Tunes Josie Franklyn

The For-Tunes at the
Old House at Home

For-Tunes at Ricky's

Paul Spooner at Ricky's

Danny Raven & Renegades 1959

Original Strangers

Johnny Rocco & the Paramounts

Nights out at Clarence Pier and the Locarno Ballroom

By 1962 vocalists and electric guitars dominated popular music. Local groups like the Diplomats, Renegades, Southern Sounds and Rebels may have set out playing instrumentals but soon featured singers Mike Devon, Danny Raven, Chris Ryder and Johnny Rocco, while local shops like Bennett's in Fratton Road enjoyed a growing trade in solid electric Fenders and Burns guitars and Vox amplifiers. On the live music scene in Portsmouth, the Savoy, Kimbells and Clarence Pier ballrooms began featuring the new beat groups alongside and increasingly instead of the older dance bands.

Adjacent to Clarence Pier, the funfair's waltzer was a key location for pop fans, hanging out to listen to the latest pop sounds. In 1963 it was shown in a BBC documentary by John Boorman called Citizen '63 which followed Portsmouth schoolgirl Marion Knight and friends dancing, singing and laughing around the youth clubs, beaches and coffee bars of the early 1960s.

In early 1963, the Top Ten featured British instrumentals at one, two and three - Jet Harris & Tony Meehan, the Shadows and the Tornados. The Shadows were the major influence on most young British musicians, then in October 1962 a new group from Liverpool, the Beatles released their first single and the pop world was transformed again.

The Savoy attracted a new audience by opening for 'juniors' on Saturday mornings, which provided another opportunity for local groups to play. Young people were enjoying themselves whether as musicians, fans or consumers of the latest fashions and music although the local (and national) media were sometimes alarmed by their behaviour.

In the spring of 1963, the Beatles appeared twice in Portsmouth and again just before Christmas by which time they were huge in Britain and about to take America by storm. In the same year fellow Merseybeat acts like Gerry & the Pacemakers and Billy J Kramer came to the city as did the Hollies, Freddie & the Dreamers and Brian Poole & the Tremeloes. In September, the Rolling Stones played at the Savoy and by the end of that momentous year many of the local groups were adding American blues, rhythm & blues and 'Motown' covers to their repertoires. The British beat boom had an enormous impact on popular music but in the clubs it was soon battling with the more earthy sounds of R&B.

At the same time, older folk and 'roots' styles contributed to an acoustic folk boom on both sides of the Atlantic – although again the 'purity' of unaccompanied singers was challenged by the sound of the guitar – albeit the acoustic guitar. British 'Trad' had enjoyed chart success in the early sixties but Kenny Ball's "Sukiyaki" was the final one, during the severe winter of early 1963. Locally, clubs like the Rendezvous and Kimbells and pubs including the Oyster House, Pure Drop and Railway continued to feature traditional jazz but a new south coast group was attracting the biggest local audiences and pointing the way to the new sound. They began as the Blues Brothers but would soon be better known as Manfred Mann.

The Rivals on ITV

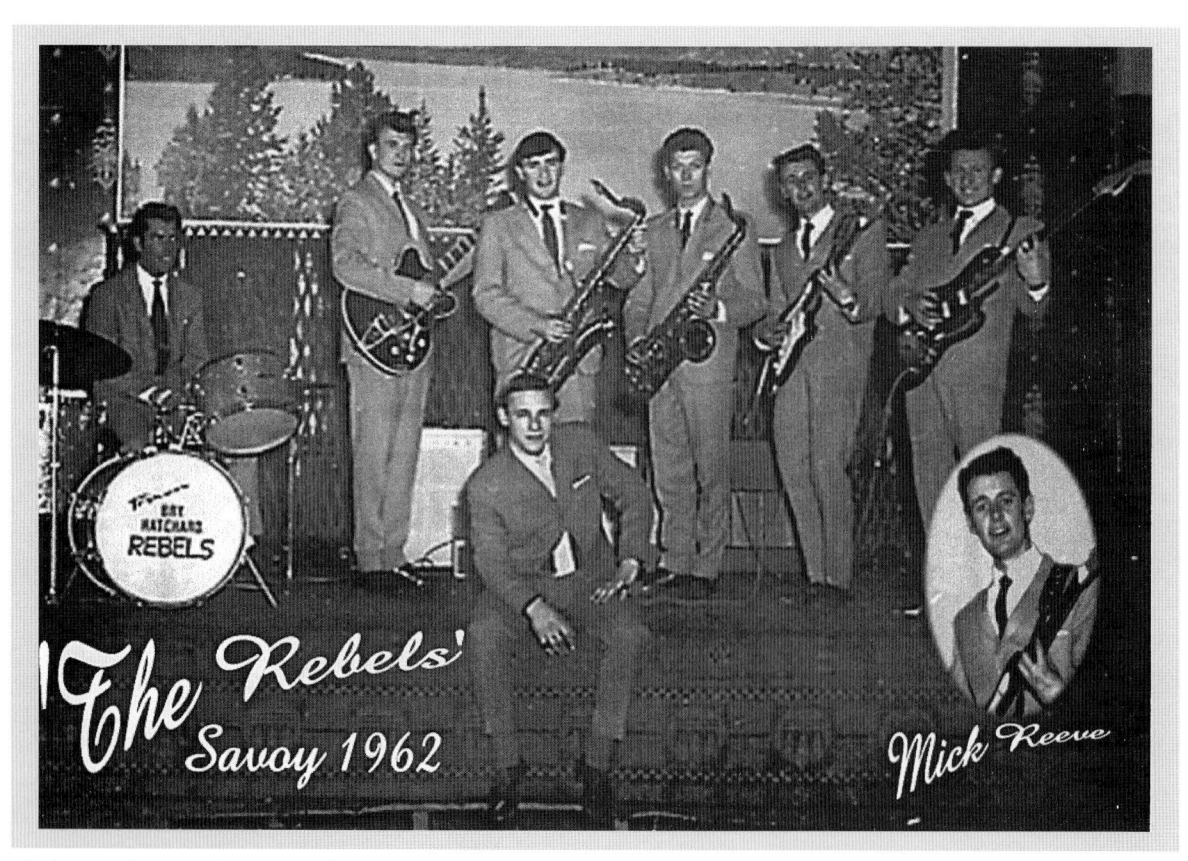

Johnny Rocco & the Rebels

The Southern Sounds at Ricky's Club 1962

Avengers at Oak Park School

The Semi Tones

The Boys at South Parade Pier

The Renegades

The Renegades

The Residents 1961

The Residents at Eastney Modern School

Residents rehearse at Copnor Secondary Modern

Residents' holiday in sunny Spain

The Furys

The Furys

The Furys at St Edmunds School

Adam Faith at
Portsmouth Guildhall

Sandie Shaw at Portsmouth Guildhall

The Honeys' tour with Helen Shapiro, Danny Williams, the Kestrels and Jet & Tony, who had replaced the Beatles

Pompey's Paul? (Brian Kemp of Five-by-Five)

Pompey Pop 65

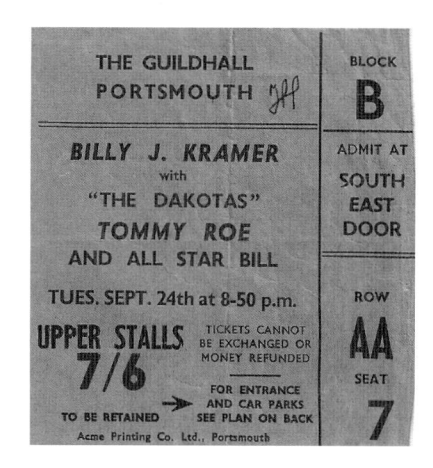

Sue's autographs

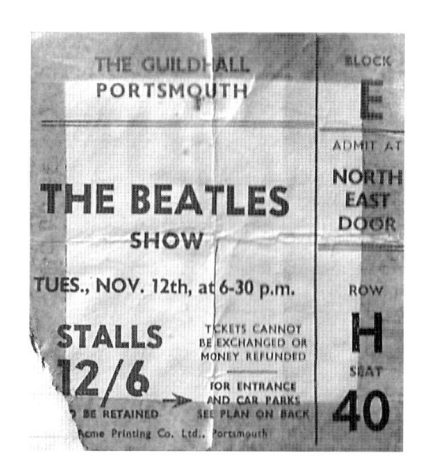

Beatles fan

Young Sue

JUNIOR ROCK AND TWIST

SATURDAY MORNINGS

TO

LOCAL ROCK GROUPS

1/-   10.30 a.m. to 12.30   1/-

Parents wishing to accompany their children,
admitted "FREE" for first four weeks

Saturday 3rd November	THE	STORMS
,, 10th ,,	,,	SOUTHERNERS
,, 17th ,,	,,	MIDNITERS
,, 24th ,,	,,	FLEETWOODS

HEALTHY RECREATION — WITH SOCIAL BACKGROUND
IN A FIRST CLASS BALLROOM

Junior Twist Savoy

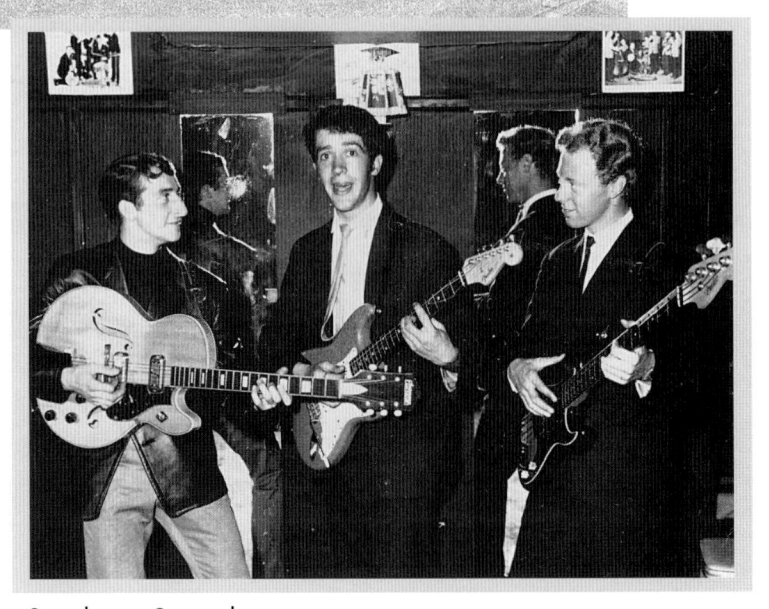

Southern Sounds

Barry & the Strollers

Barry & the Strollers

Barry & the Strollers

Barry & the Strollers at Cosham

Pompey Pop 69

The Strollers

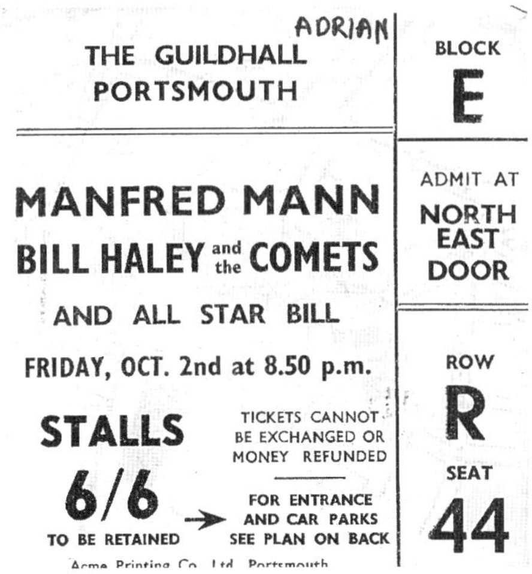

THE GUILDHALL
PORTSMOUTH
ADRIAN
BLOCK
E

MANFRED MANN
BILL HALEY and the COMETS
AND ALL STAR BILL
FRIDAY, OCT. 2nd at 8.50 p.m.
STALLS
6/6
TO BE RETAINED

TICKETS CANNOT
BE EXCHANGED OR
MONEY REFUNDED

FOR ENTRANCE
AND CAR PARKS
SEE PLAN ON BACK

ADMIT AT
NORTH
EAST
DOOR

ROW
R
SEAT
44

Acme Printing Co. Ltd. Portsmouth

MANFRED MANN STARTED IN SOUTH HAMPSHIRE INCLUDING RESIDENCIES AT THE RAILWAY AND KIMBELLS THEY TOPPED THE BILL IN OCTOBER 1964 AS BILL HALEY FINALLY ARRIVED IN THE CITY

Mike King

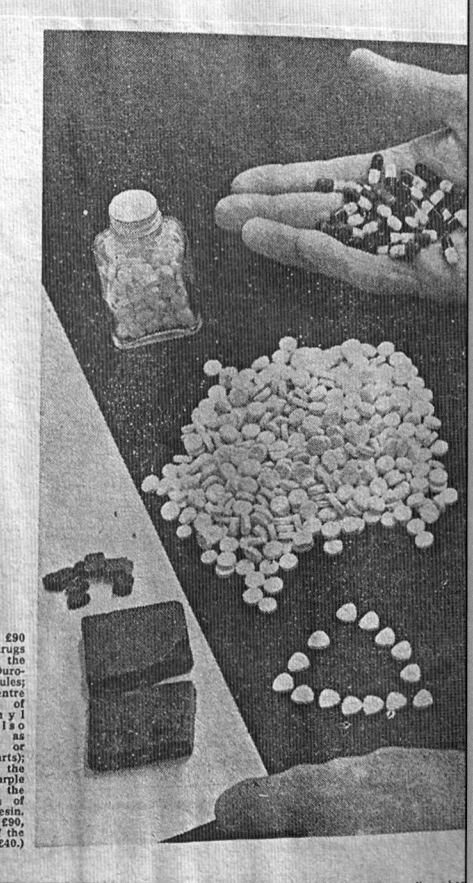

Youth Drifts

Youth in Chains

Audrey Jeans

Renegades 1961

South Parade Pier 1950s

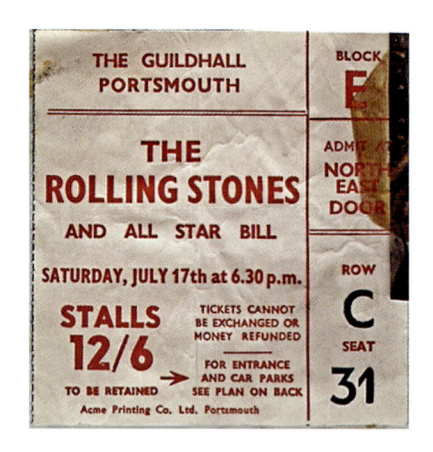

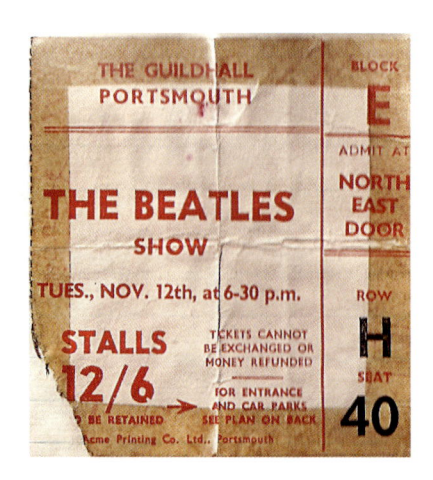

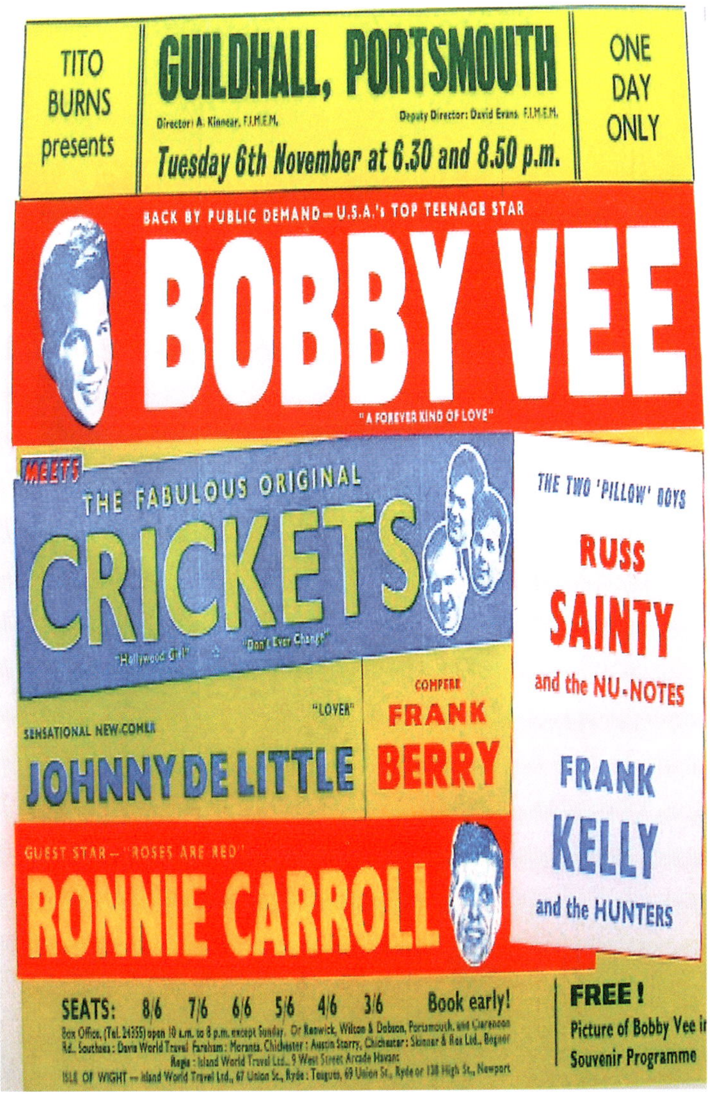
TITO BURNS presents
GUILDHALL, PORTSMOUTH
Director: A. Kinnear, F.I.M.E.M.
Deputy Director: David Evans. F.I.M.E.M.
Tuesday 6th November at 6.30 and 8.50 p.m.
ONE DAY ONLY
BACK BY PUBLIC DEMAND—U.S.A.'s TOP TEENAGE STAR
BOBBY VEE
"A FOREVER KIND OF LOVE"
MEETS
THE FABULOUS ORIGINAL
CRICKETS
"Hollywood Girl" ☆ "Don't Ever Change"
THE TWO 'PILLOW' BOYS
RUSS SAINTY
and the NU-NOTES
SENSATIONAL NEW-COMER
"LOVER"
JOHNNY DE LITTLE
COMPERE
FRANK BERRY
FRANK KELLY
and the HUNTERS
GUEST STAR—"ROSES ARE RED"
RONNIE CARROLL
SEATS: 8/6 7/6 6/6 5/6 4/6 3/6 Book early!
FREE!
Picture of Bobby Vee in
Souvenir Programme

Portsmouth Folkhouse Proudly Presents
★
A Folk Concert
Starring THE WORLD FAMOUS FOLK STAR FROM THE UNITED STATES
CAROLYN HESTER
with Supporting Artists
M.C. Jon ISHERWOOD
at the Oddfellows Hall.. Kingston Road . Portsmouth
on THURSDAY, 29th JULY, 1965 8—10.30 p.m.
DOORS OPEN 7.30 P.M.
Admission 5/-
Refreshments
Ample seating facilities

Peter White's 1962 'Strat' from Bennett's

Mike Devon & Diplomats

THE ONE IN THE MIDDLE • WATERMELON MAN
WHAT AM I TO DO • WITH GOD ON OUR SIDE
mono
HIS MASTER'S VOICE
EMI
the one in the middle
MANFRED MANN

7.30-
11.00
★SATURDAYS★
NON-
STOP
PORTSMOUTH'S "RENDEZVOUS" CLUB
RHYTHM
-AND-
BLUES
TWO GROUPS (See Local Press)
LONG JOHN BALDRY
GRAHAM BOND
ANIMALS
DOWNLINERS SECT
JIMMY POWELL ETC.
ODDFELLOWS HALL, KINGSTON ROAD
Members 5/-
JOIN NOW!
"E.S." ENTERTAINMENTS - FAREHAM

GUILDHALL, Portsmouth
Director of Entertainments: David Evans, F.I.M.E.M.
FOR ONE NIGHT ONLY—TWO PERFORMANCES ONLY
SATURDAY 22nd MAY at 6.30 and 8.50 p.m.

By arrangement with Austin Newman, Arthur Kimbrell presents —

DONOVAN
NEW FACES CHRIS CARLSEN
GUEST ARTISTES **UNIT FOUR PLUS 2**
JOHN L. WATSON and the HUMMELFLUGS

THE PRETTY THINGS

Stalls 12/6 10/6 8/6 6/6 4/6   Circle 12/6 10/6 8/6 6/6

Book at Guildhall Box Office (Telephone: Portsmouth 24355) open 10 a.m. to 8 p.m. except Sunday : Renwick, Wilton and Dobson, Portsmouth and Clarendon Road, Southsea : Davis World Travel, Fareham : Morants, Chichester : Skinner and Rea Ltd., Bognor Regis : Island World Travel, 9 West Street Arcade, Havant   On the Isle of Wight—Island World Travel, 67 Union Street, Ryde : Teague's, 69 Union Street, Ryde or 138 High Street, Newport   Postal bookings enclose remittance and stamped addressed envelope

POSTAL BOOKING SLIP
DONOVAN CONCERT
Please send _____ seats at _____ for the _____ performance on Saturday 22nd May
I enclose stamped addressed envelope and postal order cheque value _____
To _____
NAME _____
ADDRESS _____
Hastings Printing Company, Portland Place, Hastings

GUILDHALL - PORTSMOUTH
Director of Entertainments: DAVID EVANS, F.I.M.Ent.
SATURDAY 12TH JUNE AT 7.30 P.M.
Telephone 24355

THE E.F.D.S.S. presents A GREAT FOLK SONG & BLUES CONCERT with

THE LEGENDARY JOSH WHITE

FIRST APPEARANCE IN ENGLAND OF
BUFFY SAINTE-MARIE

THE REV. GARY DAVIS

Tickets from Guildhall Box Office (Tel. 24355) and usual agents

TICKETS
12/6   10/-
7/6   5/-

Hastings Printing Co.

Pompey Pop 77

The Birdcage

Cilla and Jimmy James at the Birdcage

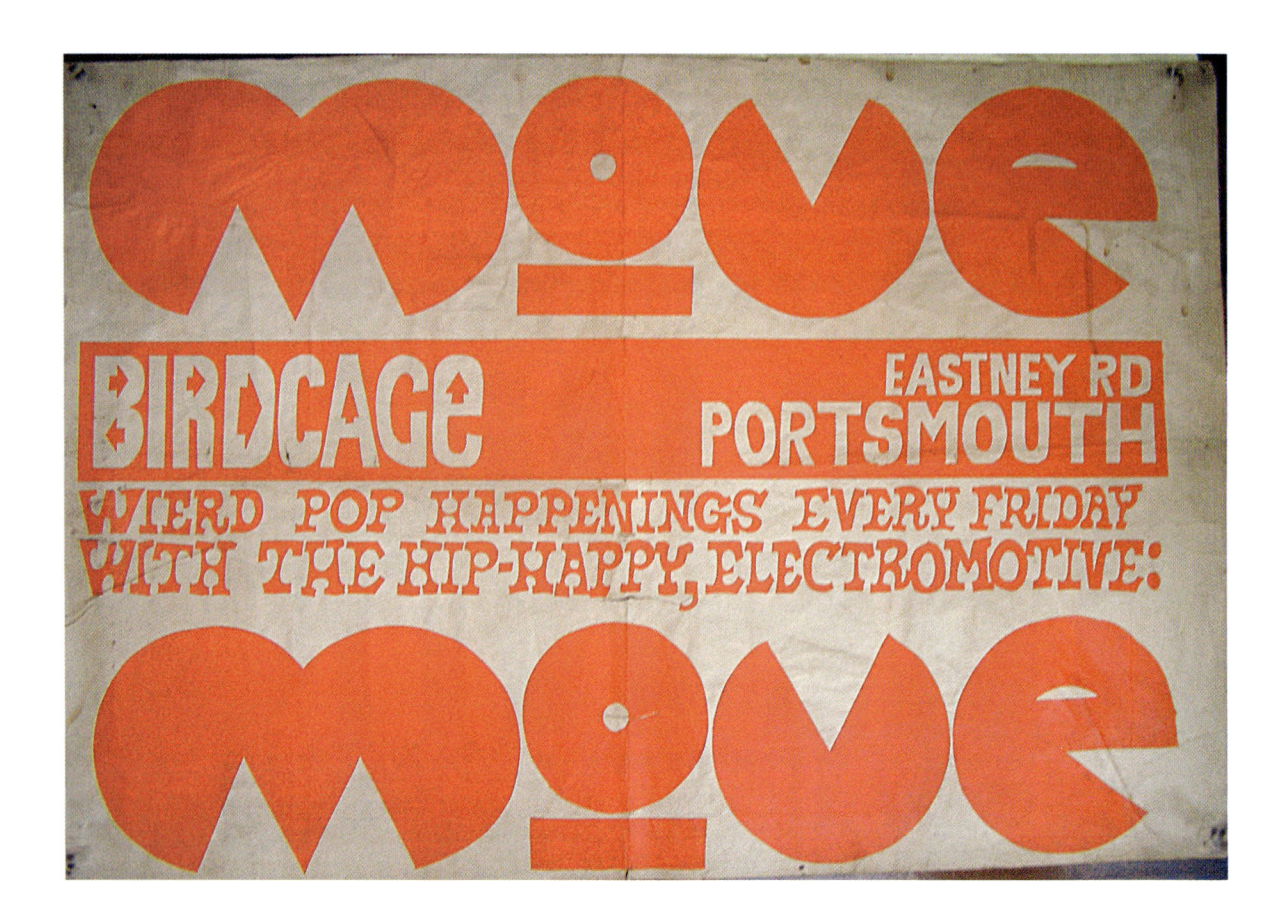

Pompey Pop   79

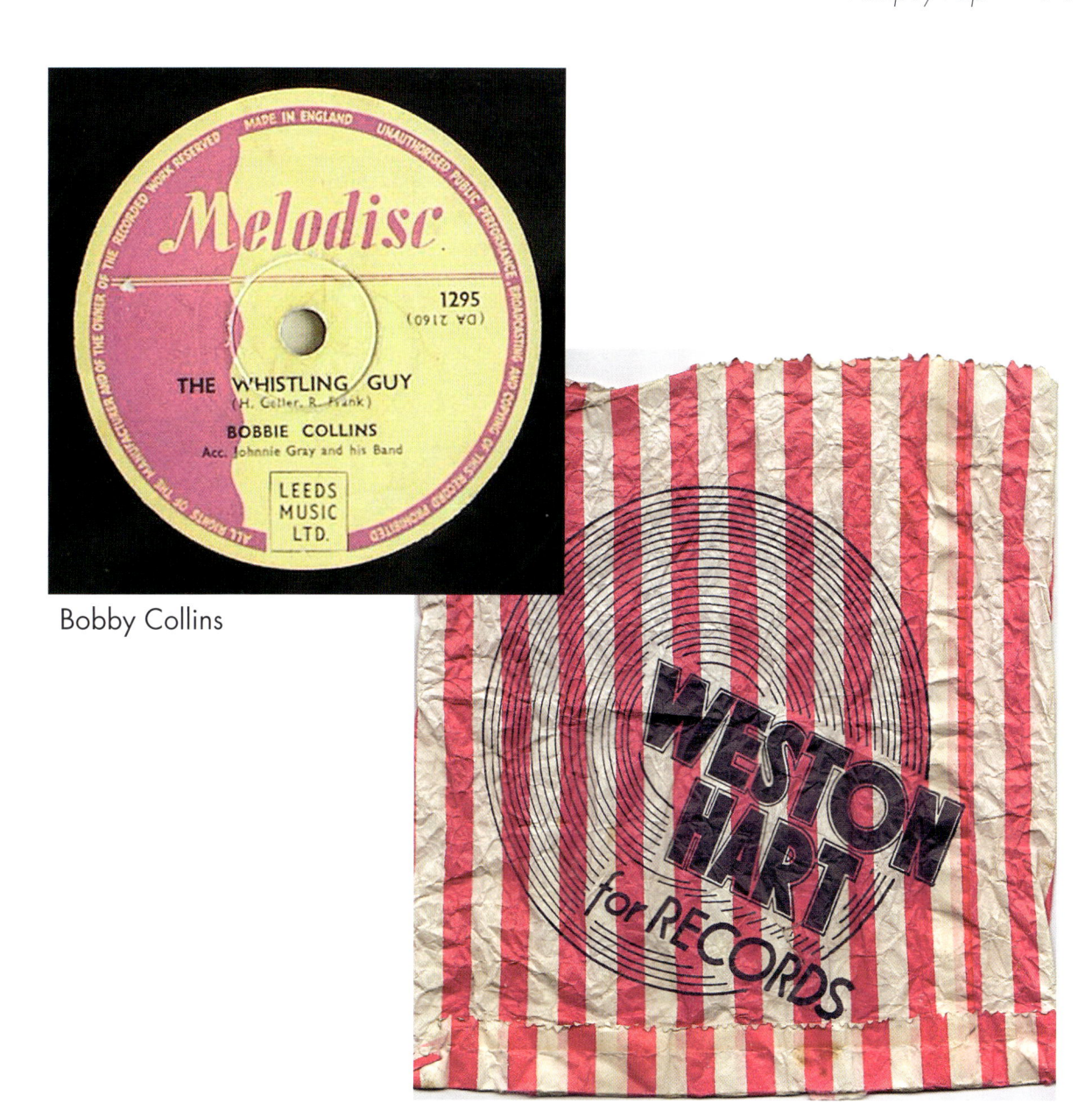

Bobby Collins

45 single bag

Frank Kelly

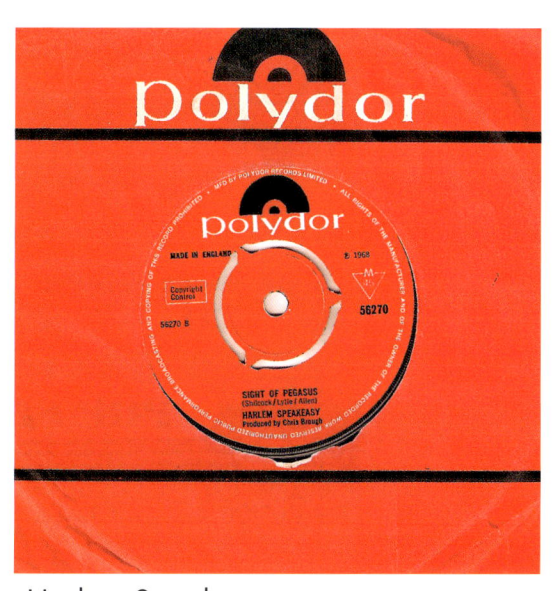

Harlem Speakeasy

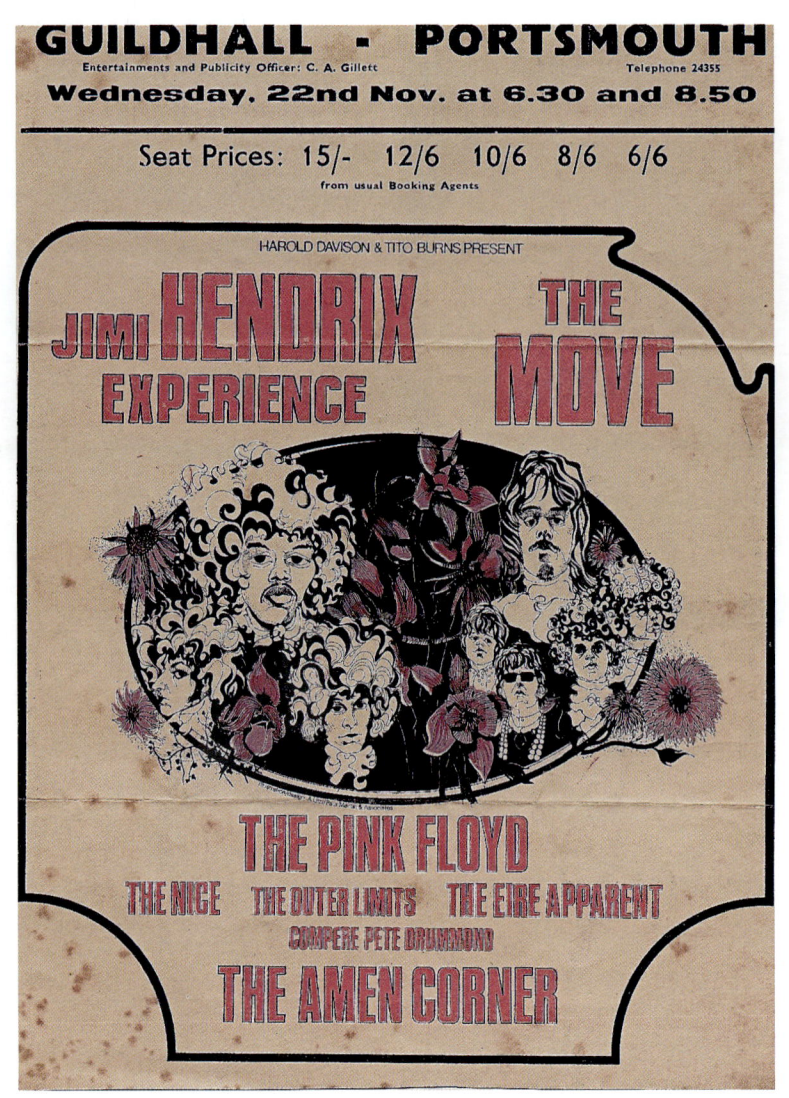

Hendrix and Floyd at the Guildhall

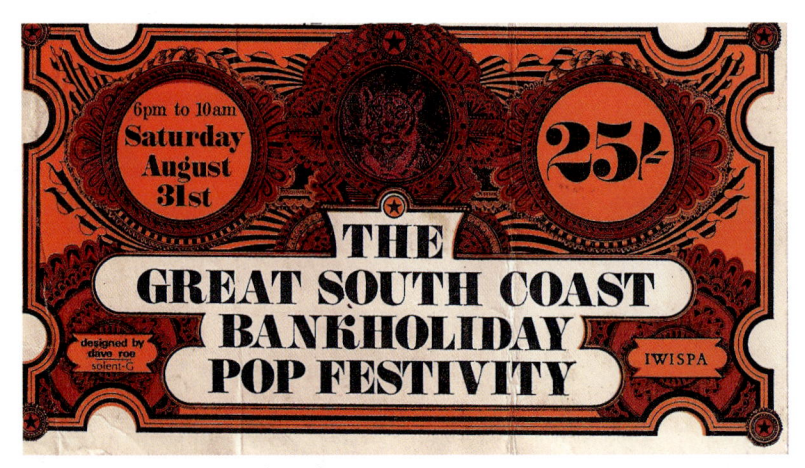

First IOW Festival Ticket

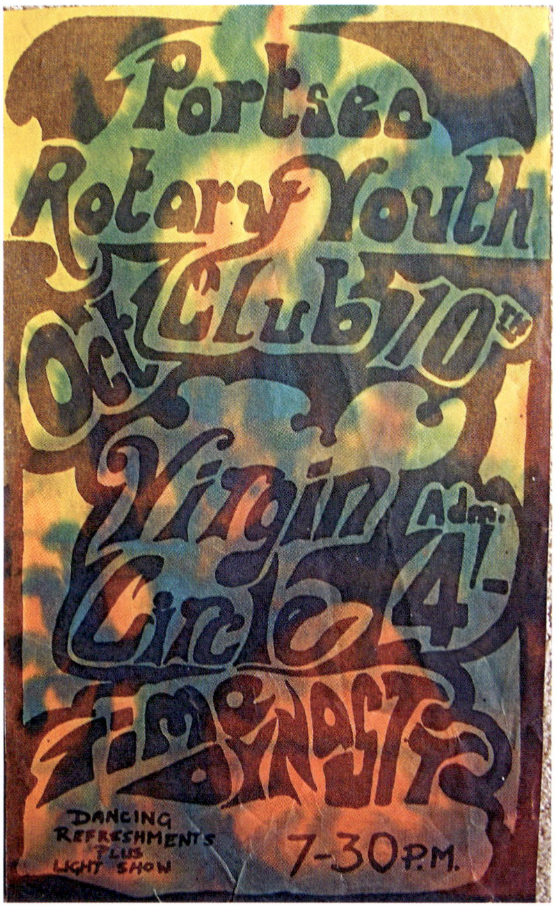

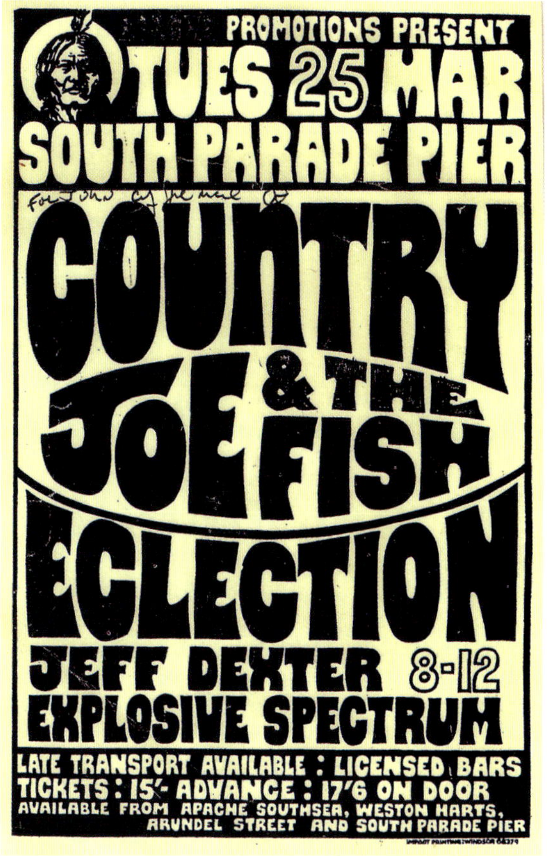

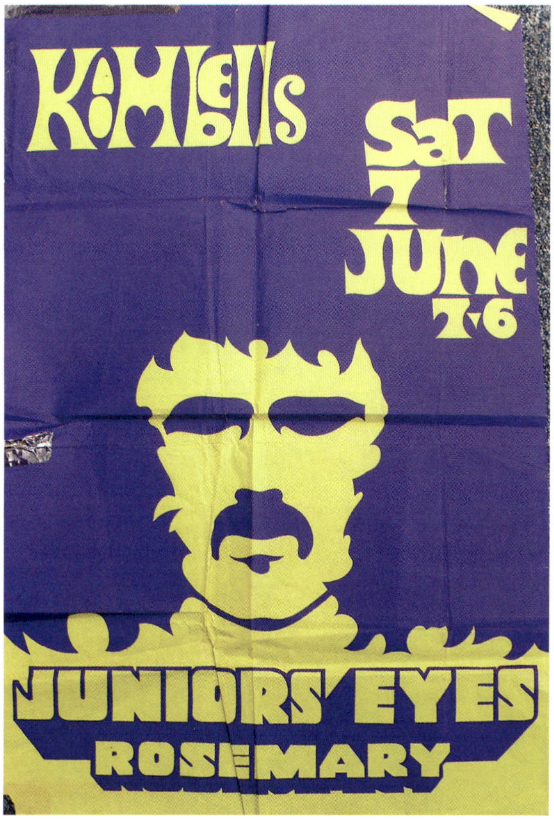

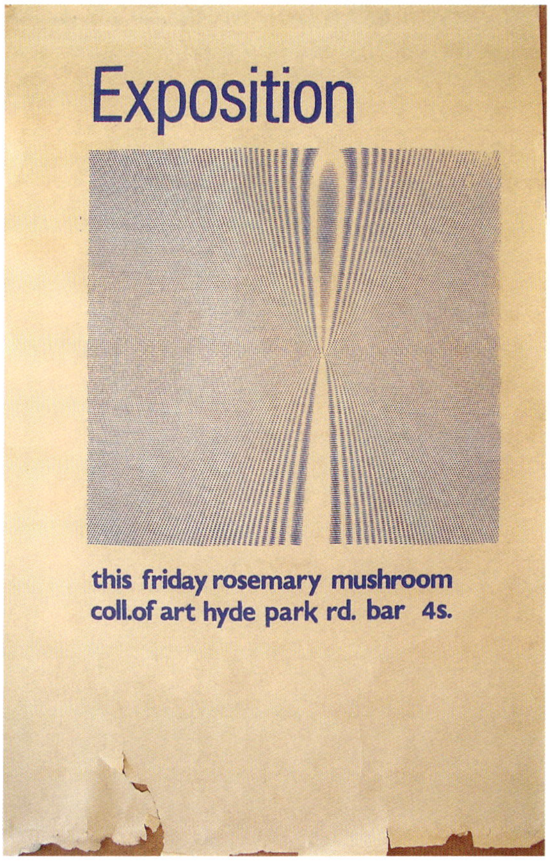

82 *Pompey Pop*

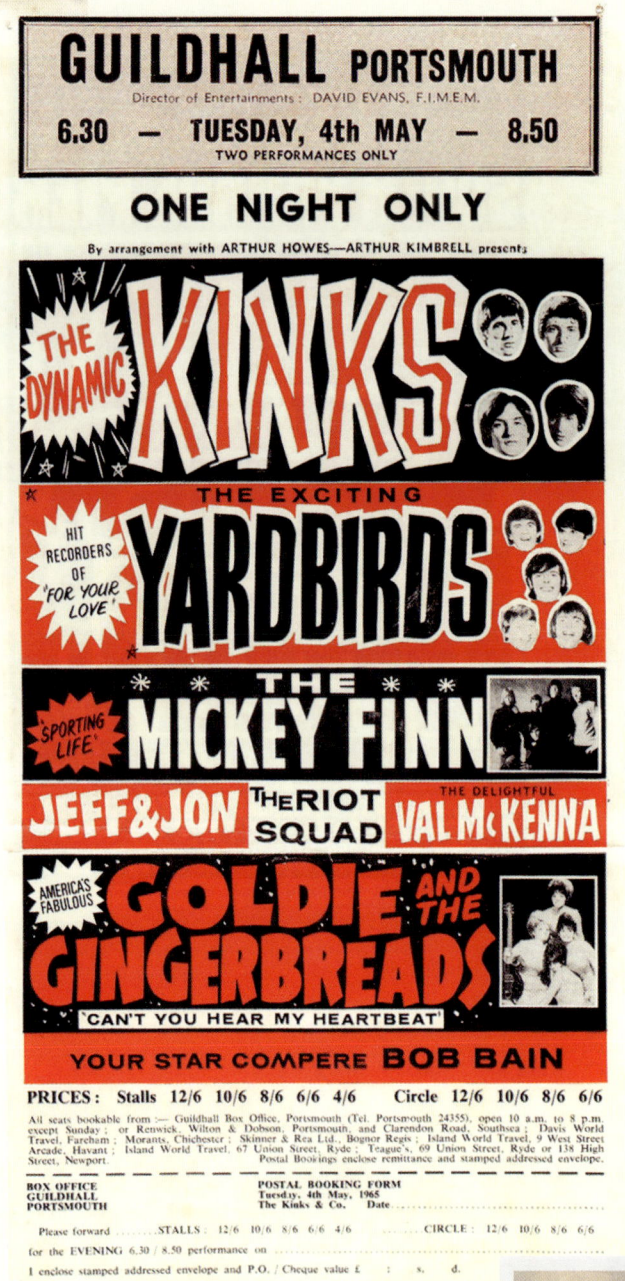

GUILDHALL PORTSMOUTH
Director of Entertainments: DAVID EVANS, F.I.M.E.M.
6.30 — TUESDAY, 4th MAY — 8.50
TWO PERFORMANCES ONLY

ONE NIGHT ONLY

By arrangement with ARTHUR HOWES—ARTHUR KIMBRELL presents

THE DYNAMIC **KINKS**

THE EXCITING **YARDBIRDS**
HIT RECORDERS OF 'FOR YOUR LOVE'

'SPORTING LIFE' **THE MICKEY FINN**

JEFF & JON THE RIOT SQUAD The delightful VAL McKENNA

AMERICA'S FABULOUS **GOLDIE AND THE GINGERBREADS**
'CAN'T YOU HEAR MY HEARTBEAT'

YOUR STAR COMPERE BOB BAIN

PRICES: Stalls 12/6 10/6 8/6 6/6 4/6 Circle 12/6 10/6 8/6 6/6

Sons of Man at the Pier

Hayling on a sunny Sunday

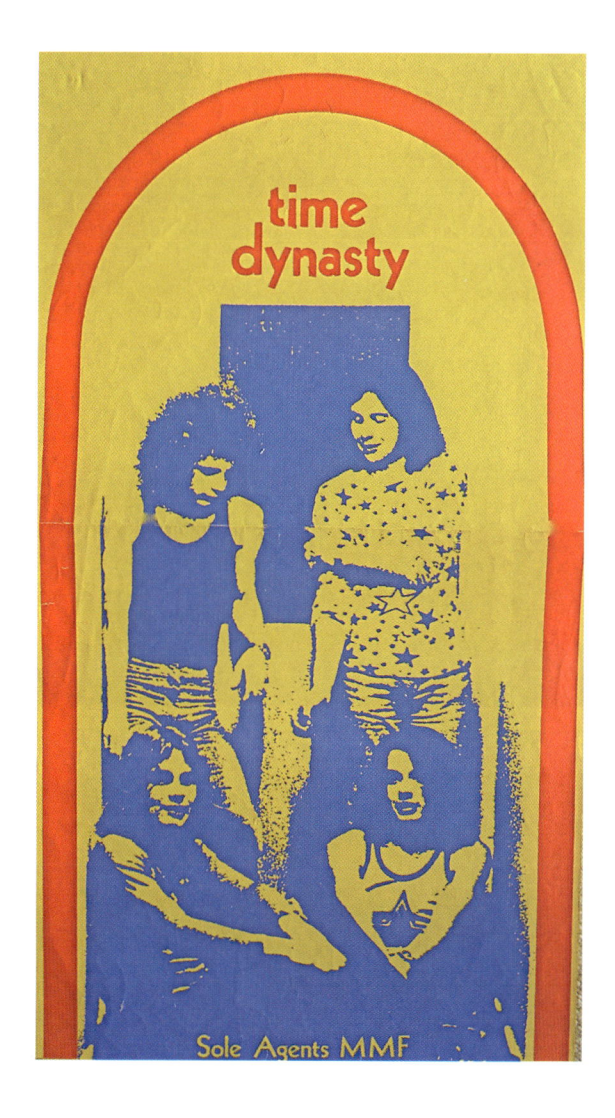

Phil Shulman

Simon Dupree including Elton John in Scotland

> Simon Dupree's keyboard player Eric Hine was taken ill prior to a tour of Scotland so the agency found a temporary replacement, Reg Dwight, who then returned to songwriting and performing under his stage name Elton John

Rikki Farr, MC at the IOW Festival 1970

ISLAND RECORDS IN ASSOCIATION WITH
APACHE PROMOTIONS
Present at South Parade Pier
on Wednesday 17th July 1968
7.30 p.m. — 1 a.m.
TRAFFIC
SPOOKY TOOTH
FAMILY
and Radio 1 D.J. John Peel
10/-
Licenced Bar   Late Transport

> Rikki Farr brought most of the great live acts to Portsmouth from 1965 at the Birdcage, Kimbells, the Pier and King's Theatre before moving on to the Isle of Wight festivals as promoter and MC

Barry & the Strollers

Pete Stroller & the Drifters

Pete Stroller & Drifters at Clarence Pier

Brothers Scarlett win at the Savoy

Brothers Scarlett at Hillside Youth Club

Brothers Scarlett

The Royals

The Third Dimension 1965

The Dynachords

The Southern Sounds

WIMBLEDON WINNERS!

by Peter Jones

JUST like the atmosphere of a Cup Final. Only more so—there were eleven different sets of fans all setting up a-roaring and a-yelling. The grand finals of the Record Mirror-sponsored "All Britain Beat Contest '65" went off violently well at Wimbledon Palais on Sunday evening.

A crowd of 3,000 jam-packed, shoulder to shoulder. Banners fluttering and falling. Roars of approval. And a near breaking-point atmosphere of tension. Tension which went on after the contest in the judges' room.

For there was, on actual marking, a dead-heat for first place. Five judges, allocating up to 45 marks per group, had (to the exact half-point) a tie between The Talismen, from Portsmouth, and Themselves, from Hounslow. The individual sections (presentation, original number, musical ability) were re-checked. And it came down to a casting vote from the judges.

CONTRACT

The Talismen (two guitars, drums, vocalist) won by a whisker. The Talismen get a contract with Decca Records, two amplifiers from Messrs. Burns (valued £200), a set of suits from West End tailor Harry Fenton, and a publishing contract with Keith Prowse Music. For Themselves, there is a recording test with Decca, plus a Burns' amplifier valued at £75. The Beltons, from Crawley, came third, and the Cosmic Sounds, from Chessington, were fourth. Both get recording tests with Decca.

Standards among the eleven competing groups were exceptionally, surprisingly, high. Good, well-varied programmes; each group was allowed twelve minutes to show their paces. Order of playing was fixed by a "lucky draw", but again one felt sorry for the Flexmen, who were drawn to open the proceedings. Again, though, someone has to start the show...

Competing groups not mentioned so far were: The Sidekicks, The Minute Men, The Barracudas, The Southbeats, The Rojeens, The M.I. 4. For all of them, it had been a long trail through the contest heats over the past few months.

Judges? Bill Phillips represented Keith Prowse Music; Dick Rowe, Decca recording manager, watched for future talent; talented songstress Barbara Kay deputised for Vicki Wickham, who was ill; Chris Roberts was there from Burns' musical instrument sales; and myself, Record Mirror.

A drama-charged evening's entertainment, all right. A tremendous success. Anybody who reckons there's a slackening off interest in beat contests should have seen this one.

RIGHT—Winning group the Talismen. They're also seen below with Mrs. Farrell, wife of Jim Farrell, one of Burns' top executives. Bottom—runners-up, Themselves (yes, that's their name!) seen here with compere Eric Corrie. (All RM pics).

The Talismen win Record Mirror

The Talismen

THE ALL BRITAIN BEAT CONTEST 1964/65
THE GRAND FINALISTS
IN ALPHABETICAL ORDER

The **BARRACUDAS**
FROM: LONDON

The **COSMIC SOUNDS**
FROM: CHESSINGTON, SURREY.

The **DALTONS**
FROM: CRAWLEY, SUSSEX.

The **FLEXMEN**
FROM: SOUTHALL, MIDDLESEX.

M.I.4.
FROM: NEW MALDEN, SURREY.

The **MINUTE MEN**
FROM: LONDON.

The **ROJEENS**
FROM: MARGATE, KENT.

The **SIDEKICKS**
FROM: HARROW, MIDDLESEX.

The **TALISMEN**
FROM: PORTSMOUTH, HAMPSHIRE.

"THEMSELVES"
FROM: HOUNSLOW, MIDDLESEX.

The **SOUTHBEATS**
FROM: BOGNOR, SUSSEX.

ALSO APPEARING
MIKE RABIN and his MUSIC

Talismen Final

The Furys & Carnival Queen

Dynamos 1963

Dynamos 1962

Dynamos 1962

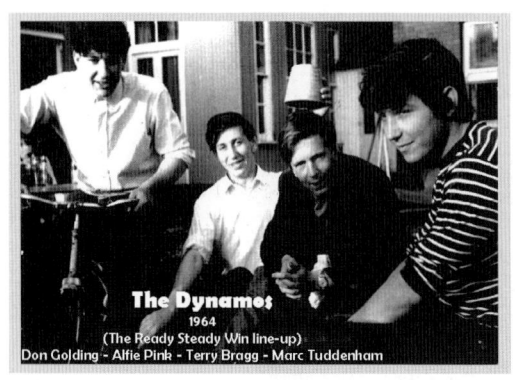

The Dynamos on ITV's
Ready Steady Win

Dynamos 1964

PORTSMOUTH'S DYNAMOS REACHED THE 1964 FINAL OF TV'S READY STEADY WIN, A SPIN-OFF FROM THE LEGENDARY READY STEADY GO. BO STREET RUNNERS INCLUDING MICK FLEETWOOD WON THE TALENT SHOW AND THE LP INCLUDED A DYNAMOS TRACK

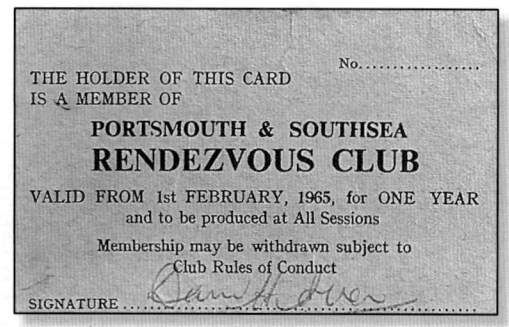

Rendezvous Card

The Concorde at Kimbells

Flyposting Ernie, Sears of the Rendezvous

Rendezvous poster

Pompey Pop 93

Kimbells membership 63

Sons of Man

Sons of Man

Sons of Man

Sons of Man

The Challengers

The Challengers and van

Snake Pit, Southsea beach

Classics with Toney Ransley on vibes

Saturday afternoon outside Verrecchias in the Guildhall Square

Rod Stewart & Robby, Osborne Rd

Rod Stewart and pals in Pompey

'Banjo' Rod on Southsea Common

Rod - Ladies Mile

Stars of the Rendezvous reunited - Rod Stewart & Emmett Hennessy

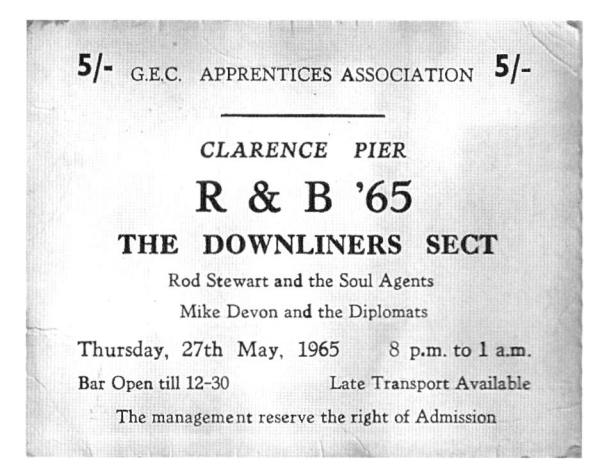

5/- G.E.C. APPRENTICES ASSOCIATION **5/-**

CLARENCE PIER
R & B '65
THE DOWNLINERS SECT
Rod Stewart and the Soul Agents
Mike Devon and the Diplomats

Thursday, 27th May, 1965   8 p.m. to 1 a.m.
Bar Open till 12-30   Late Transport Available
The management reserve the right of Admission

Rod Stewart Ticket

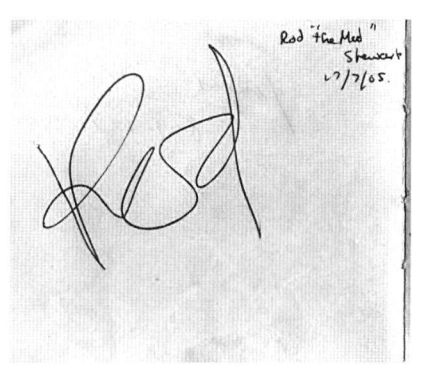

Rod "the Mod" Stewart 27/7/65.

Rod's autograph

The Storms going to Germany

The Storms

Pompey Pop 101

The Classics support David Bowie

The Classics

The Classics support Manfred Mann

Classics

Barry & Zodiacs

Dave Pittard Mod drummer

The Coastliners

Beatle-plus hairstyles

J Crow Combo

John Crow & Russ Hatchard

The Talbot Hotel

The Railway Hotel

THE BRITISH FOLK REVIVAL OF THE 1960S INCLUDED THE PORTSMOUTH AREA WHERE A NUMBER OF CLUBS FLOURISHED, MAINLY IN PUBS. INITIALLY IT SHARED ITS FOLLOWERS WITH JAZZ AND BLUES FANS AND LOCAL 'STARS' INCLUDED JON ISHERWOOD AND PAT NELSON

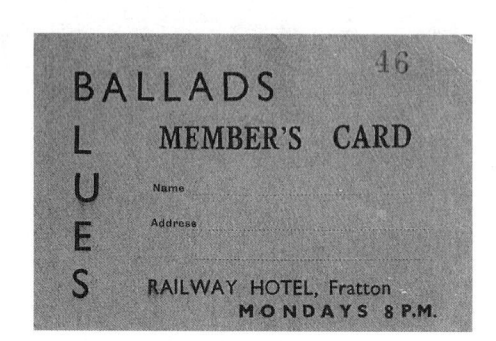

Pat Nelson & Jon Isherwood

Jon Isherwood & Ted Wenham

Barry Roberts & Ted Wenham

Country Folk

Pat Nelson

Frank Hurlock singing at the Railway

Derek Sarjeant

Jon Isherwood

Jon Isherwood

Donna & Small

Long John Baldry at the Railway

Pete Stanley & Wizz Jones, Bluegrass at the Railway

Long John Baldry

Cliff Aungier & Royd Rivers

Railway Folk Club

Railway regulars

Royd Rivers & Gerry Lockran

Pompey Pop 113

Wally Whyton & Red Sullivan at the Railway

FOLK CONCERT
JESSE FULLER
CLARENCE PIER
monday march 15
8 p.m.
malcolm price trio

Manfred Mann including Dave Richmond
(Photo by Michael Ochs Archives/Getty Images)

Mike Hugg, Manfred Mann, Mike in the Abbey Rd recording
(Photo by Jeremy Fletcher/Redferns)

Jack Bruce and Manfred Mann (Photo: Ivan Keeman / Redferns Agency)

Manfred Mann (L-R Manfred Mann, Tom McGuinness, Mike Vickers, Paul Jones and Mike Hugg) perform on the TV show Ready Steady Go, January 1964
(Photo by Michael Ochs Archives/Getty Images)

Jon Isherwood with Terry
Shulman (left) and Audrey

Donna & Steve '69

By 1965 some local groups switched from a basic guitar line-up and were adding organs and saxophones – a response to the growing popularity of black American soul and rhythm & blues. In the Portsmouth club scene this owed much initially to regular appearances by Manfred Mann and Georgie Fame & the Blue Flames – one of the finest locally was the J Crow Combo who played briefly on the London club scene.

They all played at Kimbells in Osborne Road as did Chris Farlowe, Graham Bond, Alexis Korner, John Mayall and the Yardbirds. In 1964, the Rendezvous Club moved from Southsea to the Oddfellows Hall and changed from British traditional jazz to the new rhythm & blues. The club featured some of those same acts, as well as Downliners Sect, the (original) Moody Blues and Long John Baldry & the Hoochie Coochie Men. When the latter appeared there at Christmas 1964, Baldry did not arrive and his second singer led the band. He had spent some 'beatnik' years around Portsmouth and this may have been his first 'solo' spot. His name was Rod Stewart. Among the American blues singers who appeared in the city were Muddy Waters, John Lee Hooker, Little Walter, Rev Gary Davis, Sister Rosetta Tharpe and Josh White.

In February 1965 boxer's son Rikki Farr arrived in Portsmouth and teamed up with locals Robin Beste, Pete Boardman, Bob Beard and others to launch the Birdcage Club at Kimbells. In August it moved to a permanent home in Eastney and for the next two years dominated the local mod scene, presenting the Who, Small Faces, Wilson Pickett, Ike & Tina Turner, the Action and Jimmy James & the Vagabonds. The Birdcage was featured in the cover photos and sleeve notes to the latter's first album New Religion.

The Savoy and Guildhall were more mainstream pop in this period with the latter featuring the typical pop packages. Elsewhere, smaller clubs and youth clubs catered for younger audiences, coffee bars and boutiques flourished and Portsmouth had its own lively version of the 'swinging sixties'. Nonetheless, the Savoy continued to present dance bands of the pre-rock & roll style and while that audience grew older and went out less decline did not lead to disappearance.

The Guildhall featured some modern jazz artists – including the MJQ and Duke Ellington while similar sounds could be heard in pubs like the Cambridge (Southsea) – including Tony Crombie who returned with organist Alan Crombie. Traditional jazz was less prominent but the folk scene was growing in strength around two local 'stars' – Jon Isherwood and Pat Nelson and other performers like Barry Roberts, Barry Gordon, the Cumberland Echoes, Donna and the Loft Folk Four. Visitors ranged from Ewan McColl to Paul Simon.

The Rendezvous did not survive the competition from the Birdcage but one of the local bands who played regular support spots there, the Roadrunners, recruited the Classics' rhythm section, changed their name to Simon Dupree & the Big Sound and won a recording contract which would take them to the Top Ten – the only entirely Portsmouth area group to achieve that feat. Other local groups enjoyed some success – the Dynamos were finalists in ITV's Ready Steady Win, the St Louis Checks reached the final of the Melody Maker's national competition, although only the Talismen went on to win – a national event at Wimbledon reported in Record Mirror.

By the mid-1960s popular music was the focus of a variety of scenes around the city from the sharpest mods to their deadly rivals the rockers (with their own Southsea coffee bar). Those of bohemian spirit followed folk and jazz, while mainstream music and fashions were found in places like the new Locarno in Arundel Street. In addition we began to realise that popular music was not a teenage fad but something people grew up with and continued to enjoy in different ways. This was helped by the expansion of radio in Britain.

Birdcage Mods

The Action at the Birdcage

Scooter boy

PORTSMOUTH HAD A THRIVING MOD SCENE IN THE MID-1960S, CENTRED ON THE BIRDCAGE CLUB, EASTNEY WHICH FEATURED ALL THE MAJOR LIVE ACTS FROM BRITAIN AND MANY AMERICAN VISITORS

Herbie Goins at the Birdcage

Pompey Pop 119

Groovy chicks

Robin Beste of the Birdcage

Eastney's Birdcage

Jimmy James & the Vagabonds at the Birdcage

BIRDCAGE EASTNEY RD. PORTSMOUTH

Thur 19 Jan Geno Washington and the RAM JAM band

Fri 20th DISC NITE

Sat 21 the KNACK

Sun 2 DISC NITE

SAT. 18 DEC 7·15-11: the, pop-art, guitar smashing epic (my generation)

the WHO

now open Sunday afternoon 3-5-30

DONT MISS OUR XMAS AND NEW YEAR RAVES

COMING IN '66 SOLOMAN BURKE LITTLE STEVIE WONDER THE DRIFTERS and many more

Pompey Pop 121

BIRDCAGE
EASTNEY RD. PORTSMOUTH
SATURDAY 25th.
ALL NIGHTER
CHRIS FARLOWE
PLUS THE ACADEMY

RIKKI'S BIRD CAGE
EASTNEY ROAD . PORTSMOUTH
JUNE 24th . 8-12 ONLY 6/-
THE
ACTION
JULY 8th — JOHN MAYALL
JULY 15th — PROCUL HARUN
ALNITER

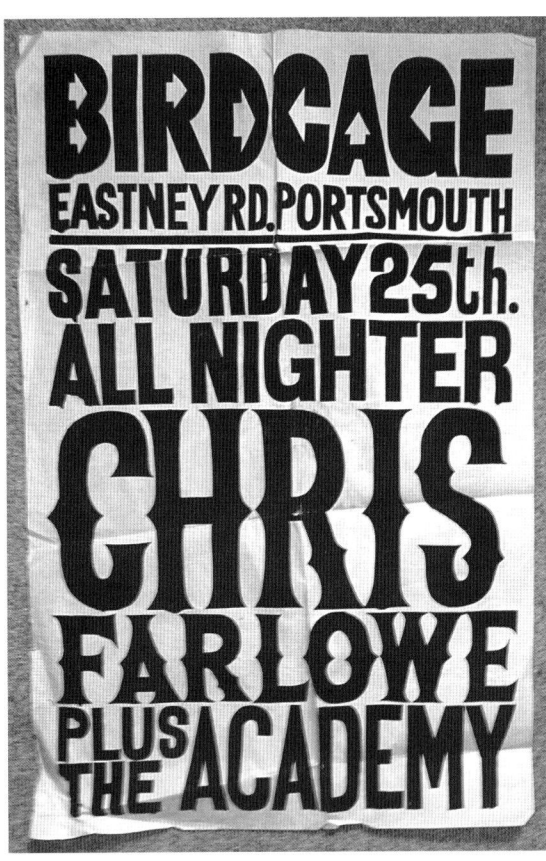

UNDER NEW MANAGMENT
BLUE LAGOON
KIMBELL'S BALLROOM ★
PORTSMOUTH
SATURDAY 23 JULY
HALF NIGHTER!
7/6 before 9 P.M.
CHRIS FARLOWE
new coffee lounge

Portsmouth
RENDEZVOUS CLUB
Oddfellows Hall · Kingston Road

SATURDAY 28th AUGUST

Direct from the recent "Stones" Tour

THE BOZ PEOPLE!

with the new popular
SOUL SOCIETY

MEMBERS 5/-   MEMBERSHIP 1/-

Holiday snap

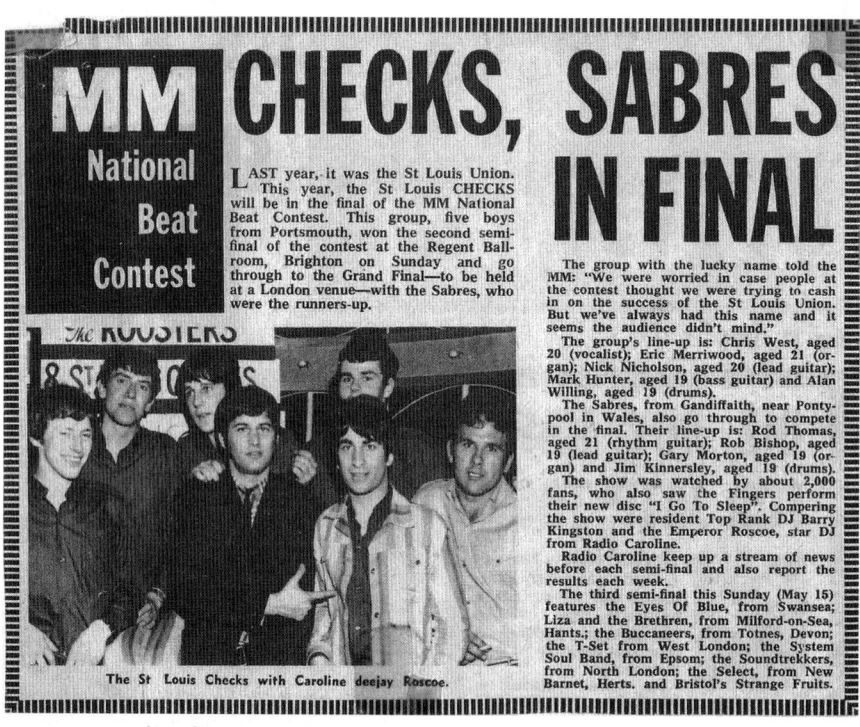

St Louis Checks in Melody Maker

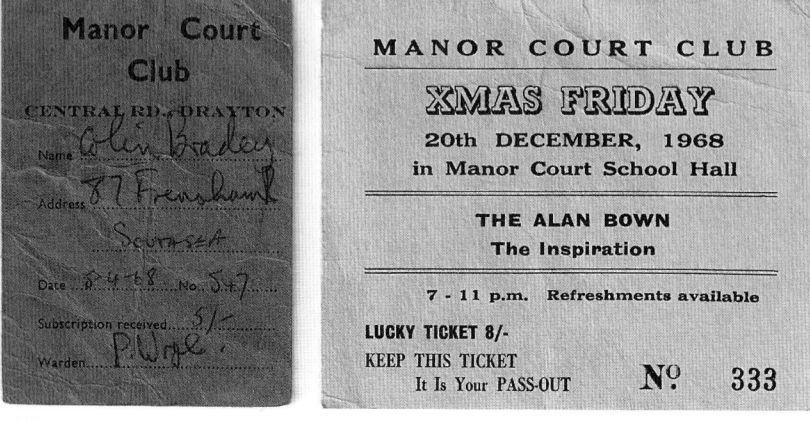

Manor Court

St Louis Checks

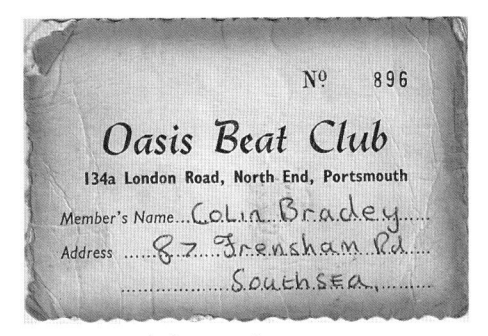

Oasis Club card

St Louis Checks' Chris West

St Louis Checks, Rock Gardens Pavilion

Pompey Pop 125

Inspiration

Rampant

Klimaks

Klimaks' Graham Barnes

Klimaks at the Shoreline Club

Klimaks at the Shoreline Club

The Academy

Mark Barrie Four

The Monk at the Brook Club

The Monk in the Rock Gdns

Morgan's Camel Train

The (original) Soul Society

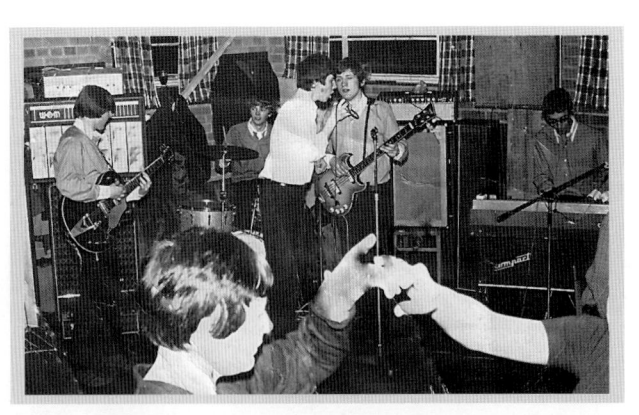

Travis Raymar

Soul Society at the Tricorn

Soul Society entertain the students

Simon Dupree & the Big Sound

Simon Dupree & the Big Sound

Simon Dupree & the Big Sound

Simon Dupree & the Big Sound

Pompey Pop   131

Simon Dupree & the Big Sound

Simon Dupree & the Big Sound

The Teapots at Kimbells with Dorreen Parsons (left) of the Indigo Vat

The Teapots

The Wrong Direction

In December 1966 Cream appeared at the Birdcage, followed a month later by Pink Floyd, including Syd Barrett and light show. Some mods adopted brighter colours and longer hair as psychedelia, American 'West Coast' sounds and British blues made their impact across the country – even before the release of Sgt Pepper and the 'Summer of Love'. In the local 'paper, Spinner's weekly column was an early champion of acts like Love and Captain Beafheart.

Nonetheless soul bands and sounds remained popular locally at the Marina Club (Ricky's) and with Inspiration, Image (from Soul Society) and Harlem Speakeasy who in 1968 turned professional and released a Polydor single "Aretha" – a Drifters cover. Sadly it failed to sell while Cherry Smash also released singles without success. However, in 1967, "Kites" by Simon Dupree & the Big Sound reached the British Top 10.

It was said that they did not like the record but it was their biggest hit and an example of pop-psychedelia then growing in popularity. By the end of 1967, the legendary Birdcage Club had become the Brave New World booking acts like the Who, Family, Ten Years After and Julie Driscoll as well as folk, jazz and cabaret acts. The mix did not really work and by 1969 it had been converted to the Pack Night Club. Rikki Farr went back to Southsea, promoting psychedelic, blues and progressive acts at South Parade Pier and Kimbells. He also opened his Apache boutiques in Southsea and at the Tricorn, and from 1968 was MC and one of the promoters of the three Isle of Wight Festivals.

North End's Soul Parlour became the Parlour and booked local bands and recording acts like Free, Skip Bifferty and Blossom Toes. The finest days of the local youth clubs were at Manor Court, which regularly featured visitors like Alan Bown and the Amboy Dukes plus local support acts.

The News reported alarms and court cases about the latest illegal drug, LSD. By the late 1960s, the students at the College of Technology (now the University), College of Art, College of Education and Highbury Technical College were increasingly active in the promoting of live gigs around the city. One major event in May 1968 was the students' "Dance of Words" across the whole ground floor of the Guildhall, featuring poets, jazz musicians and newer rock acts like Free and Fairport Convention.

Coconut Mushroom – perhaps the first local group to perform American 'West Coast' sounds - played at the "Dance of Words" and later signed with Apple. Tangerine Slyde followed a similar sound and played gigs at London's legendary Middle Earth Club before reforming with members of Harlem Speakeasy as Rosemary. They signed and recorded with Warner Chappells while the Universal Trash Band became Heaven and recorded an album in Denmark Street. Sadly, not one of these initiatives led to a record release – only a second, very different version of Heaven produced an album Brass Rock on CBS.

The students led experimental events at the Arts Workshop – on one occasion with Tyrannosaurus Rex and John Peel. The sixties concluded with Southsea Common's first free concert, organised, funded and featuring various local bands. These days the council runs such events on Pete Clutterbuck's beautiful bandstand.

Ricky's Club became the Marina – one of the first regular 'discos' in the city – the Locarno continued to offer mainstream 'pop' or the Jack Hawkins Orchestra and the building of the Tricorn included a night club/disco. The Guildhall continued to offer a broad range of popular music acts from Englebert Humperdink to Jimi Hendrix.

134 Pompey Pop

Blackout

Blackout on stage

The Black Cats 1964

> MANY GOOD GROUPS AND MUSICIANS CAME FROM GOSPORT. THE BLACK CATS BECAME BLACKOUT, THEN GOLD DUST AND SMILING HARD. GROUP MEMBERS SUBSEQUENTLY PLAYED WITH QUEEN, DURAN DURAN AND OTHER MAJOR ACTS

Gold Dust

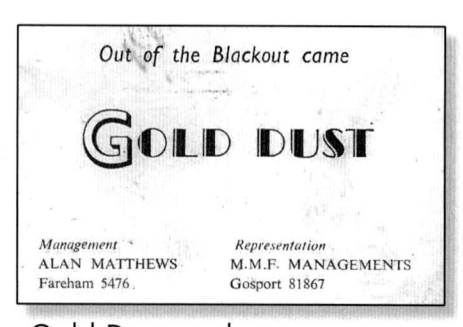

Gold Dust card

Blackout with dance duo Crimson Ballet

Blackout 1965

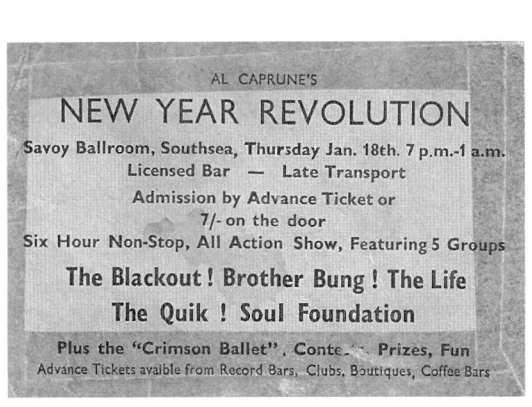

AL CAPRUNE'S
NEW YEAR REVOLUTION
Savoy Ballroom, Southsea, Thursday Jan. 18th. 7 p.m.-1 a.m.
Licensed Bar — Late Transport
Admission by Advance Ticket or
7/- on the door
Six Hour Non-Stop, All Action Show, Featuring 5 Groups
**The Blackout ! Brother Bung ! The Life
The Quik ! Soul Foundation**
Plus the "Crimson Ballet", Contests, Prizes, Fun
Advance Tickets avaible from Record Bars, Clubs, Boutiques, Coffee Bars

Savoy Ticket

The Parkas' First Gig

The Parkas 1967

Pompey Pop   137

Jamie's Kin

MANOR COURT CLUB
EASTER DANCE
THURSDAY 11th APRIL 1968
in Manor Court School Hall

| The Amboy Dukes | Harlem |
| The Groovy Kind | Speakeasy |

7 - 11 p.m.   Refreshments available
LUCKY TICKET 4/-
KEEP THIS TICKET
It Is Your PASS-OUT   N⁰ 113

Manor Court ticket

Jamie's Kin at Kimbells

Rivals' singer Gren Mayes

The Inspiration

Harlem Speakeasy at the
Red Door Club

Harlem Speakeasy

XMAS BONANZA
BRAVE NEW WORLD
EASTNEY ROAD, EASTNEY, SOUTHSEA

SATURDAY, DEC. 23rd, 7.30 - 12.00
FROM U.S.A. LUCAS, WITH THE MIKE COTTON SOUND

SUNDAY, DEC. 24th, 7.30 - 11.00
The ERROL BRUCE SOUL PARTY + The HARLEM SPEAKEASY
XMAS EVE PARTY NIGHT. PRIZES, COMPETITIONS

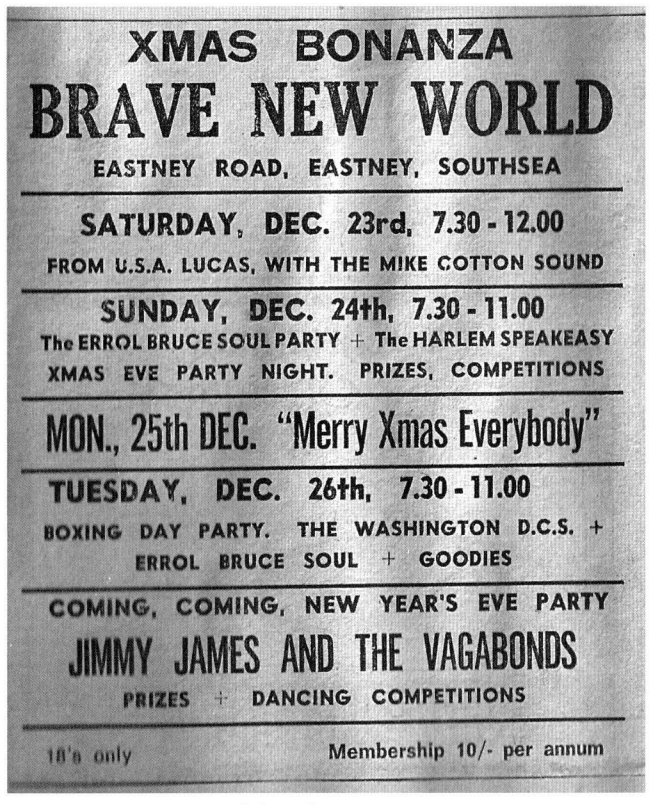

MON., 25th DEC. "Merry Xmas Everybody"

TUESDAY, DEC. 26th, 7.30 - 11.00
BOXING DAY PARTY. THE WASHINGTON D.C.S. +
ERROL BRUCE SOUL + GOODIES

COMING, COMING, NEW YEAR'S EVE PARTY
JIMMY JAMES AND THE VAGABONDS
PRIZES + DANCING COMPETITIONS

18's only   Membership 10/- per annum

Brave New World, Christmas 1967

Image

Apache

Coat design

Fur coat with high, stand up collar has brown leather insets; bands above cuffs; and bolero style inset in bodice which has two buckle fastenings.

Crimson ballet

Crimson Ballet

Linn - 'The Bird' DJ who also ran the (Soul) Parlour

Brother Bung at the Indigo Vat

Brother Bung at the Indigo Vat

Pevensey Brown Melon

Bernie Fox of Blues Convention

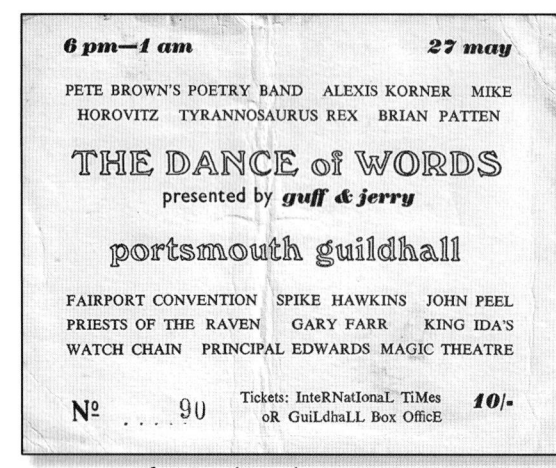

```
6 pm—1 am                          27 may
  PETE BROWN'S POETRY BAND   ALEXIS KORNER   MIKE
  HOROVITZ   TYRANNOSAURUS REX   BRIAN PATTEN

           THE DANCE of WORDS
              presented by guff & jerry
            portsmouth guildhall

  FAIRPORT CONVENTION   SPIKE HAWKINS   JOHN PEEL
  PRIESTS OF THE RAVEN     GARY FARR    KING IDA'S
  WATCH CHAIN   PRINCIPAL EDWARDS MAGIC THEATRE

  No ... 90    Tickets: InteRNatIonaL TiMes    10/-
               oR GuiLdhaLL Box OfficE
```

Dance of Words ticket

> BY THE LATE '60S, STUDENTS WERE INCREASINGLY IMPORTANT AS PROMOTERS AND CONSUMERS OF POPULAR MUSIC, WHILE MUSICIANS EXPLORED BLUES, PSYCHEDELIC AND EARLY PROGRESSIVE STYLES 'DANCE OF WORDS' WAS AN EXPERIMENTAL PERIPATETIC EVENT.

Whiskey River

Cherry Smash 1967

San Cella Sound & Rikki Martin

Coconut Mushroom

Coconut Mushroom

Coconut Mushroom at the Tricorn

Light Program lightshow

Lightshow

Art students Geoff Allman and Martin Richman started Portsmouth's major lightshow and appeared at most local venues including major gigs at the Pier. Both pursued successful careers in art & design

Penny

Tangerine Slyde at the Pier

TANGERINE SLYDE APPEARED A NUMBER OF TIMES AT LONDON'S 'UNDERGROUND' CLUB "MIDDLE EARTH" AND LATER FORMED THE CORE OF ROSEMARY.

Tangerine Slyde at Stweek (Rag Week)

Rosemary at the Art College

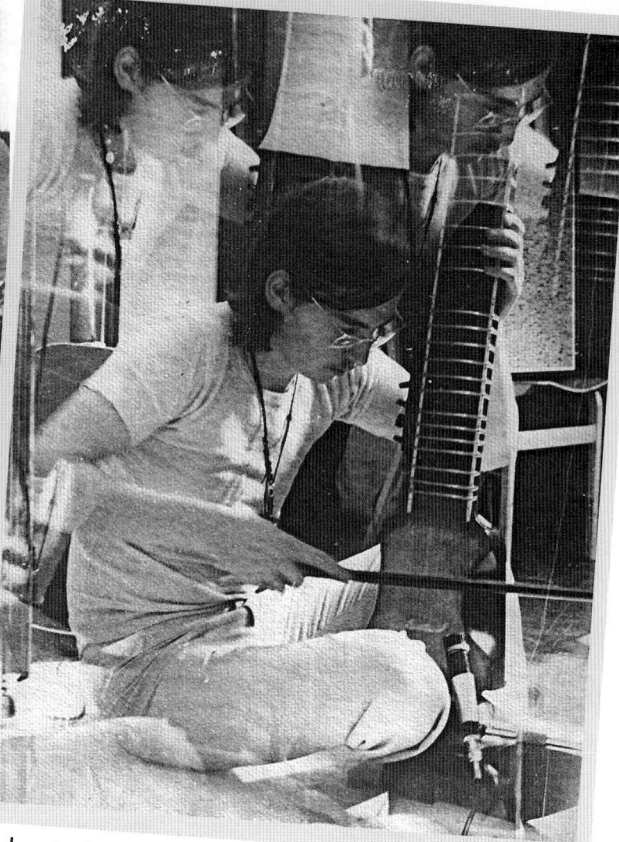

John Lytle of Rosemary

Rosemary

Rosemary at the common Free Concert 1969

Pompey Pop 149

Absence on the common

In Grandma's Absence

Hells Angels benefit Waterlooville

Absence on the common

In the Audience

Heaven on stage

Heaven

Heaven

Heaven recording at Southern Sounds in Denmark Street

Heaven Mark 2 of *Brass Rock* LP

Phil Freeman, Image, at Tricorn Xmas party

Colours; Sinah Warren

Tipner Greyhound Stadium Music Festival 1970

Pompey Pop 153

Nigel Grundy

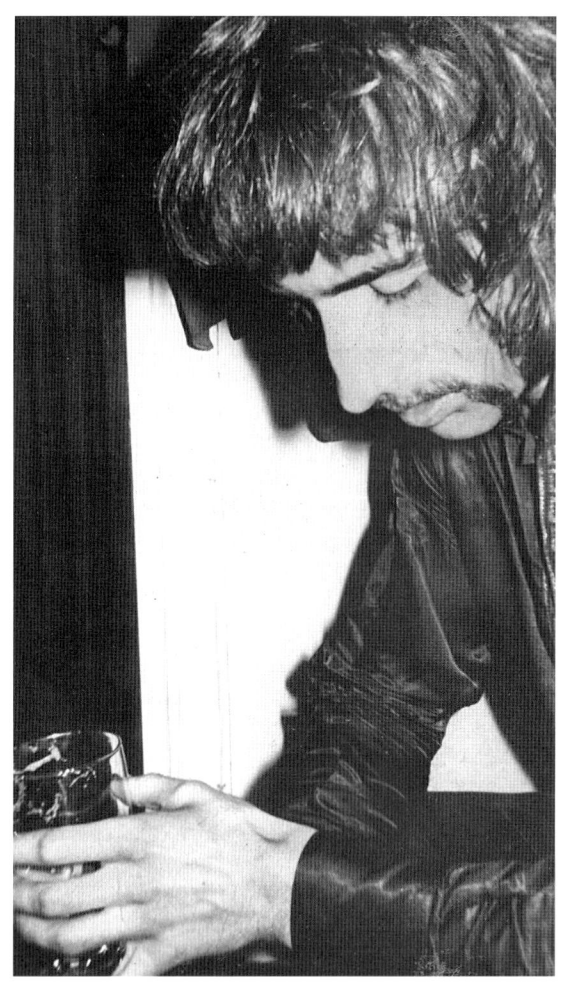

Arthur Brown, Portsmouth Guildhall

NIGEL GRUNDY GREW UP IN PORTSMOUTH WHERE HE DOCUMENTED THE LOCAL SCENE IN THE LATE 60S AND EARLY 70S, INCLUDING MAJOR ACTS AT THE PIER, GUILDHALL AND ELSEWHERE HE TAUGHT PHOTOGRAPHY AT THE UNIVERSITY AND PUBLISHES ON THE PAINTER WL WYLIE

Nigel's Press Pass

Black Sabbath at the Pier

Edgar Broughton Band, in the Pier's Dressing Rooms

Pompey Pop   155

Family at Brave
New World

Ginger Baker with his Airforce at the Pier

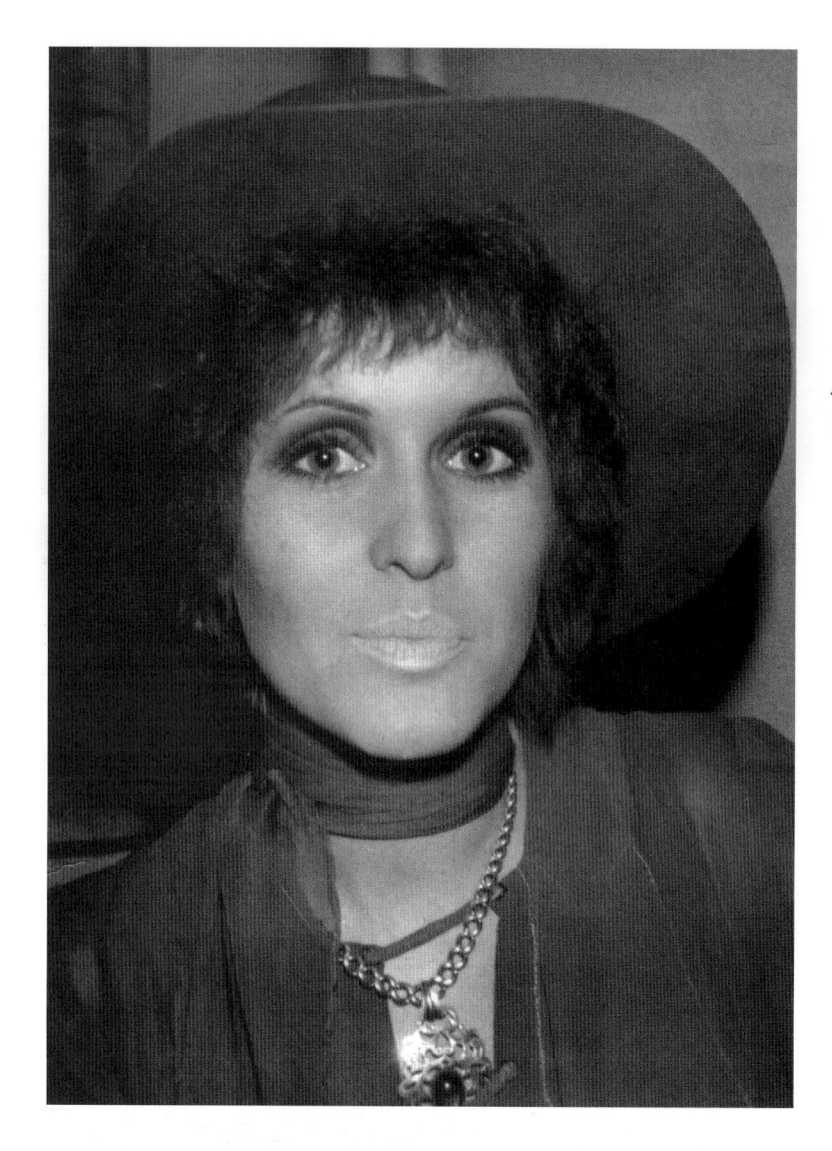

Julie Driscoll,
Portsmouth Guildhall

Gentle Giant at
Trident Studios, London

Idle Race at South Parade Pier

Pink Floyd in the Pier's Dressing Rooms

Sandy Denny and Fotheringay at the Pier.

In addition to his photographs of major acts, Nigel has provided images of local performers throughout the book including Brother Bung, Jon Isherwood, Phil Freeman, St Louis Checks, Tangerine Slyde and the Tipner Festival.

http://www.imagesafloat.com/

The Bonzo's Viv Stanshall at the Pier

The 1960s ended with a number of local rock bands performing at Kimbells while around the city the older traditional dance events were still running as they had done in previous decades. There was folk music at the Jug of Punch and the Guildhall was still booking bigger acts in concert.

On the other hand, a number of local groups like Coconut Mushroom, Heaven, Cherry Smash, Rosemary and Aubrey Small saw their dreams come and go, Simon Dupree reformed as Gentle Giant and a number of venues closed or, like the Savoy, moved from live entertainment towards discos.

This final section shows a few of the 1960s musicians continuing to play in the following decade. Some went on to greater success including Mick Feat (Mushroom) who played with Van Morrison, Spike Edney (Smiling Hard) who has played with Queen for some years and Kev Gilson with Duran Duran.

Around the corner the next generation was waiting to take our places – from Portsmouth - most notably Joe Jackson, and everywhere the punks. That's another story that has already been told splendidly from the local perspective by Tony Rollinson.

But the impact of those days has lived on in many ways and in lots of cases people are still playing. The Challengers were reunited in 2010 and Danny Raven & the Renegades in 2011. Less predictably, Woodstock star Country Joe McDonald who had played at South Parade Pier with his Fish in 1969, came back to Southsea in 2001, made it his base for a British tour with Reet Petite & Gone and appeared again on the Pier and at the seafront's Bandstand.

In 2010 the City Museum held a major exhibition called the "Birth of British Rock". It centred on the photographs of Harry Hammond but included photos and memorabilia from Portsmouth in the 1950s and 1960s. Many fans and local musicians contributed and this 'Pompey Pop' project developed from it and has flourished since. This book is the latest outcome of that work but we hope not the last.

As we were in the final stages of preparing this book, guitarist Colin Quaintance died. He was there in the very early days with the Cadillacs and subsequently the Southern Sounds. In the period after the one covered in this book, he continued to perform locally and even in his final days was still playing most weeks with his old pals. He was a deeply loved local musician and almost typical of the Pompey scene in that he was talented enough to have made it on a broader scene but for whatever reasons that didn't happen. Many local musicians have similar tales to tell but today we are able to look back with a sense of pleasure and gratitude that we lived through a magical period in a wonderful place. Thanks Pompey.

Aubrey Small at the Pier

Aubrey Small

Gilbey Twyss

The Generation

High Society

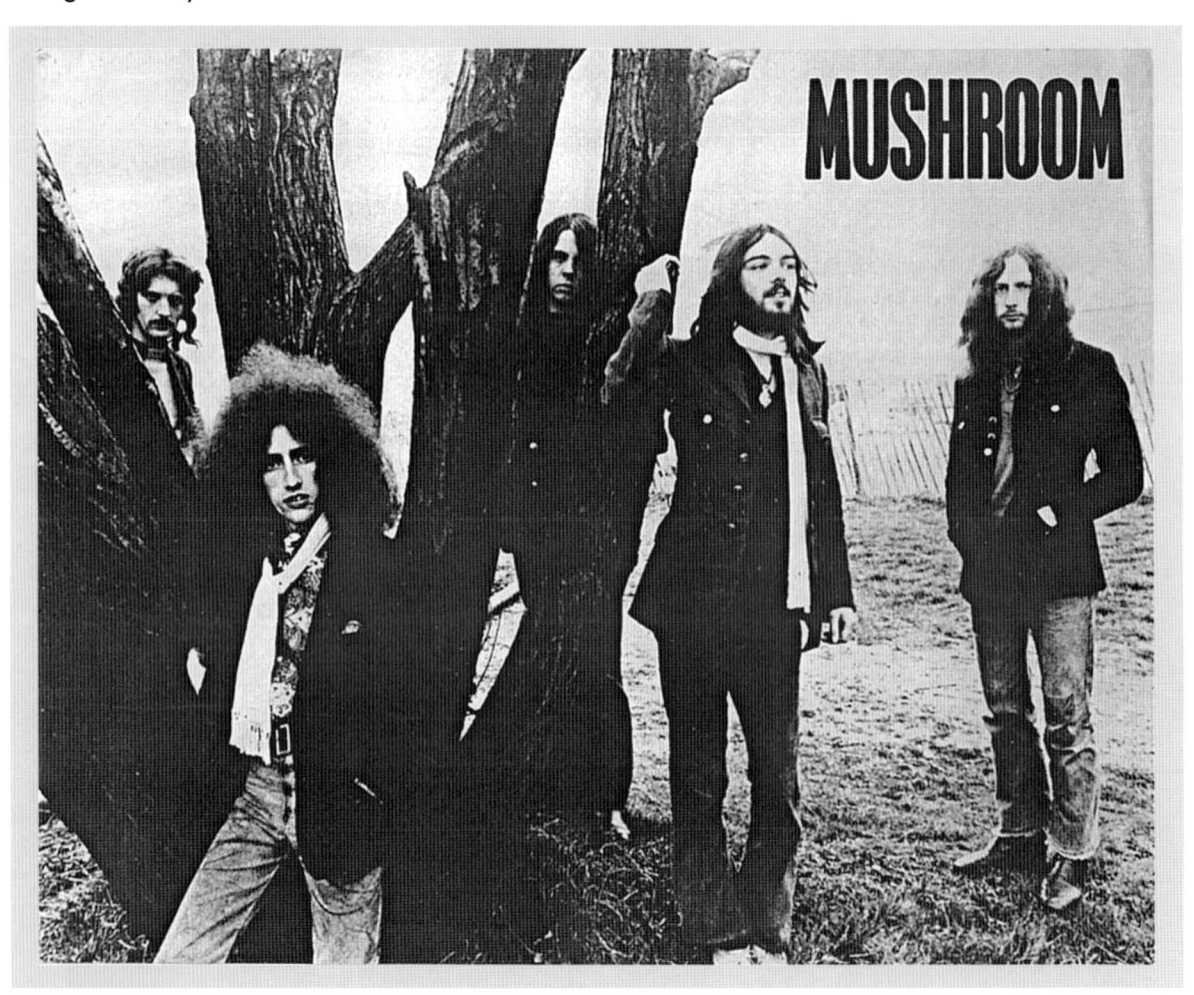

Mushroom

Smiling Hard

Springhill

The Rivals 1972 Pier's Gaiety Bar

Country Joe & Reet Petite & Gone, Southsea Bandstand 2001

Challengers reunion 2010

Danny Raven & Renegades reunion 2011

Honeys 2009

Live Five at the City Museum 2010

Cadillacs, Renegades Mick and two Daves, Kings Theatre 2010

Cadillacs, Renegades, Dynamos, Christmas 2010

For-Tunes reunion

Cresta Bob & Dave 2010

Pompey Pop 169

Two Strollers

Two Parkas & Trevor

John Clarke celebrates his birthday

Dave Barber with Helen Shapiro

Alan Christmas & Rod Watts

Mick, Phil Shulman and Dave

172   Pompey Pop

Alan (St Louis Checks) Linn (Parlour, DJ Bird) and John (Soul Society) with Mick & Lenny T

Portsmouth City Museum 2010 "The Birth of British Rock"

Hayling's Russ Sainty with Cliff

Savoy site

Kimbells site

Empress site

Oddfellows site

Ricky's site

Railway Hotel site

King's Theatre

> The Wedgewood Rooms was once the Co-op Hall. That venue, the Theatre Royal and the King's Theatre in Albert Road are rare examples of venues that still operate as such in Portsmouth. Most local venues have either changed use or disappeared completely.

Wedgewood Rooms

GROUP DIRECTORY

This list includes all the groups, dance and jazz bands portrayed in the book. Wherever possible we have listed personnel, including changes. Updates, amendments and details of other groups from the period can be found at: *www.pompeypop.co.uk*

ABSENCE: Eddie Bance (V), Colin Wagg (V), John Roberts (LG), Nigel Mills (LG), Andy Mills (D). Formerly EXP and In Grandma's Absence

ACADEMY: Marc Tuddenham (G/V), Graham Barnes (BG), Rod Watts (K), Graham Hunt (D/V).

AUBREY SMALL: Alan Christmas (V/G), Marc Tuddenham (V/G), Pete Pinckney (G/V), Rod Taylor (K/V), Dave Yearley (BG), Graham Hunt (D)

AVENGERS: Gerry Elmes (V), Mick Eveleigh (V/G)

BARRY & STROLLERS: Barry Gladding (V), Barry Fowler (G), Colin Wood (BG) replaced by Dave Gladding (BG), Pete Connor (G), Richard Baker (D), Dave Mussell (K), Barry Shute (D), Bernie Morley (LG)

BARRY & the ZODIACS: Barry Davies (V), Gerry Chandler (G), Archie Chandler (BG), Mick Primett (LG), Dave Pittard (D)

BERT PARKER & PETER HICKS: BILLY STORM & the STORMRIDERS: Billy Storm (Bertrand Parker - V), Barry Roberts (G), Terry Bragg (BG), George East (G), Percy Hall (D)

BLACK CATS/BLACKOUT: Kev Gilson (V/G/S/K), Dave Gilson (G/T), Tony Gilson (BG), Bill Carlton (G), John McLeod (K), John Jenkins (D). Became Gold Dust/ Smiling Hard

BLUES CONVENTION: Bob Pearce (V/G), Denny Barnes (G), Dave Arthur (BG) replaced by Nigel Baker (BG), Bernie Fox (D)

BOYS: Dave Rowlands (guitar), Terry Harding (bass) and others

BROTHER BUNG: Bob Pearce (V/G), Bob Gorman (G), Kevin Francis (BG), Roger Chantler (D) - from Southampton but Pearce played with Blues Convention & Chantler played once with Harlem Speakeasy. Gorman, Francis and Chantler became Fresh, recording two albums on RCA

BROTHERS SCARLETT: Dave Diapes (LG), Harry Diapes (G), Brian Diapes (BG), Bert Diapes (D). For a time they were the Brothers Scarlett plus vocalists Gary (Alan Knight) & Lee (Derek Knight). Gary & Lee left mid-60s and the group continued

CADILLACS: Merv Skidmore (V) replaced by Ricky Silver (Jimmy Stafford – V), Colin Quaintance (G/V), Patrick Green (G), Colin Wood (BG) replaced by Keith Milton (BG), Bryan Hatchard (D)

CHALLENGERS: Arthur Potts (V/H) replaced by Hughie Colgan (V), Roger Pattison (LG), John Bowes (BG), Chris Pearcy (G), Brian Davey (D)

CHAPTER SIX: Pete Bugg (V/G), Dave Pittard (D) and others

CHERRY SMASH: Bryan Hug (V), Mick Gill (G), Mark Tuddenham (G), John Curtis (BG), Bryan Sebastian (?), Graham Hunt (D).

CLASSICS: Paul Spooner (V), Ian Grant (aka Ian Duck, G), Peter O'Flaherty (BG), Tony Ransley (D), Lenny Woods (G), Simon Clifford (K).

COASTLINERS: Bob Downs (G), Mick McGuigan (BG), Alan Williams (D) plus occasional vocal trio: Ritchie Peters, Dawn & Danni

COCONUT MUSHROOM: Colin Carter (V), John Clark (G) replaced by Barry Paul (G), Roger Griffin (G), Graham Barnes (BG) replaced by Mick McGuigan (BG) replaced by Mick Feat (BG), Terry Threadingham (D). Subsequently called Mushroom

COLOURS: Pete White (V/LG), Bryan Baker (BG), Ray Baker (V/RG), Ted Ball (D) replaced by Ricky Seimark (D)

CRESTAS: Frank Kelly (V), Chris Ryder (V), Lynn Orchard (Lynn Appleton - V), Dave Field (BG), Tony Hutchins (G) replaced by Denny Newton (G), Gill Hutchins (G), replaced by Dave Thistle (G) Bob Hammond (D).

DAVE HART COMBO: Dave "Digger" Hart (G/V) and others

DEMONS SKIFFLE GROUP: Paddy Pead, John Offer, Derek Turner, Norman Allen

DENVER FOUR: Pat Green (G), Dave 'Digger' Hart (D) and others

DIPLOMATS: Geoff McKeon (LG), Keith Francis (G) replaced by Tony Smith (G), Colin Wilkinson (BG), Bob Harrigan (D) replaced by Terry Wiseman (D). Originally instrumental quartet until vocalist Mike Devon (Mike Beacon) joined - became Mike Devon & the Diplomats

DYNACHORDS: Don Bonzer (V), Adrian Bartholemew (LG), Vern Rogers (B), Jock McLeod (RG/V), Tony Hennen (D).

DYNAMOS: Marc Tuddenham aka Marc James (G/V), Don Golding (G) replaced by Roger Barber (G), Terry Bragg (BG), Tony Daws (D) replaced by Alfred Pink (D)

FIVE-BY-FIVE: Brian Kemp (B/V), Mike King (D) and others

FOR-TUNE$, a.k.a. ORIGINAL FOR-TUNE$: Josie Franklin (Veronica Lake – V), Tony Wyell (Paul Spooner – V) replaced by Ritchie Peters (Peter Richardson – V), Ron Hughes (LG), Dave Cawte (BG), Mick Cooper (K), Ken Hughes (D)

FRANK KELLY & the HUNTERS: Frank Kelly (V), Tony Hutchins (G), Dave Loney (G), John Randall (BG), Trevor Williamson (D)

FREEMEN: vocal group, Stuart Muggridge, Brian Muggridge, Alf Grainger

FURYS: Colin Skidmore (aka Dale Morris V) replaced by Ann ?, Pete White (LG), Bryan Baker (BG), Ray Baker (RG), Colin Marchant (G), Brian Hare (D), became Blue Sand, then the Colours

GARY HAYMAN TRIO: Gary Hayman (P), Terry Wiseman (D) plus one

GILBEY TWISS: Dave Allen (V), Denny Barnes (G), Mick Legg (BG), Bernie Fox (D), Mick Tuck (TS)

GENERATION: Dave Mussell (K), Steve Farrow (LG), Roger Tice (BG), Phil Briggs (D)

GENTLE GIANT: Derek Shulman (V/S), Ray Shulman (BG/G/V), Phil Shulman (TS, Tr), Gary Green (G), Kerry Minnear (K), Martin Smith (D) replaced by Malcolm Mortimore (D) replaced by John Weathers (D)

GOLD DUST: Kev Gilson (V/G/S/K), Tony Gilson (BG), Spike Edney (K), Dave Houghton (D). See Blackout

HARLEM SPEAKEASY: Jon Edwards (V), Dave Allen (V/S), Keith Shilcock (G), Geoff Gunson (BG) replaced by Mick Legg (BG), John Lytle (K), Pete Gurd (Tr), Phil Jones (S), Sam Eddings (D) replaced by Alan Williams (D)

HEAVEN: Andy Scarisbrick (G), Brian Kemp (V/BG), Mick Cooper (K), Ray King (S), Ray 'Ollie' Holloway (S), 'Nobby' Glover (D), Dave Gautrey (Tr). A second version emerged in 1970 with King, Gautrey & Glover from this group and Terry Scott (V), Eddie Harnett (G), Derek Sommerville (TS), John Gordon (BG). They released the album *Brass Rock* (CBS)

HI FI'S: (1957). Ron Monger (G), Dave ? (BG), Clyde Warren (G?), Tony Bailey (V), Dave Mears (Vibes), Tony Hart (D)

HIGH SOCIETY: 'Digger' Hart (G/V), Pete Jackson (BG/V), Keith Hawtin (D/V)

HONEYS: Anita, Pearl & Vilma Liddell vocal trio. Formerly the Liddell Triplets

HOT RODS: Eric Smith (V), Colin Quaintance (G), Ian McKeon (G), Colin Wilkinson (BG), George East (G), Bob Harrigan (D) or Johnny Witt (D)

IMAGE: Phil Freeman (V), Phil Jones (S), Alan Medland (S), Steve Grant (D) and others

IN GRANDMA'S ABSENCE: Eddie Bance (V), Colin Wagg (V), John Roberts (LG), Nigel Mills (LG) Andy Mills (D) 1968 - Became Absence

INSPIRATION: Colin Carter (V) replaced by Al Golding (V), Graham Chapman (G) replaced by Dave Clark (G), Pete Tucker (G), Brian Kemp (BG/K), Roger Tice (BG), Keith Durant (D)

JAMIE'S KIN: Nigel Baker (G), Barry Sutton (G), Pete ?? (BG), Ken Keane (BG), Mick Cooper (K), Cliff Stafford (aka Ricky Silver V/S?), Jim Handley (D)

J CROW COMBO: Mick Snowden (V) replaced by Chris Ryder (V), John Crow (S), Colin 'Mojo' Bucket (G), Larry Nicholas (K) replaced by Rufus Stone (K), Colin Wood (BG), Graham Hunt (Drums)

JOHNNIE & the CUTTERS: Dennis Gates (V), Ted Thorne (LG), Mick Reeve (G), Brian Deluchi (BG), John Coates (D)

KLIMAKS: Mick Snowden (V), Mick Rowe (LG), Graham Barnes (BG), Alan Dodds (D)

LIVE FIVE: Barry Barron (G), Dave Barber (BG), Chris Harvey (G), Mike Orton (G), Terry Wiseman (D)

MANFRED MANN: Paul Jones (Paul Pond - V/H) replaced by Mike D'Abo, Mike Vickers (G/S), Dave Richmond (BG) replaced by Tom McGuiness (BG, then G), Jack Bruce (BG), Manfred Mann (K), Mike Hugg (Hug – D/Vib)

MARK BARRY FOUR: Barry Fowler (G) Steve Stevenson (LG), Peter Hicks (BG), Jeff Smith (D)

MICK GLOVER GROUP: Mike Glover (V/G), Barry Barron (G), Dave Barber (BG), Mike Orton (G), Terry Wiseman (D) then later Glover with Steve Stevenson (G), Tony Seall (BG/DB), Alan Songhurst (D)

MIRKWOOD: Pete Bugg (V/G), Rick Buckingham (BG), Dave Mussell (KB) and others

MONK: Arthur Stevens (LG), Malcolm McInnes (V/RG), Terry Stevens (BG), Geoff Collinge (D), Tony Troy (K)

MORGAN'S CAMEL TRAIN: Ken Cornish (V), John Clark (G), Mick Legg (BG), John Pratt (D), replaced by Robbie Clarke (D)

MUSTANGS: Keith Boyes (V), Alan Clarke (G), Mike Kimber (G), replaced by Tony Nabbarro (G), Gary ? (G), Eddie Collinson (G)

ORIGINAL STRANGERS: Billy 'Nick' Nicholson (G), John Harper (D) and others

PARAMOUNTS: David Loney (LG), John Randall (BG), Tony Ransley (D) replaced by Trevor Williamson (D). At various times featured vocalists Gary & Lee (see Brothers Scarlett) and Johnny Rocco

PARKAS: John Summerfield (G/V), Robb ? (BG), Keith Summerfield (D). Still playing as Limited S

PETE STROLLER & the DRIFTERS: Pete Stroller (V), Steve Stevenson (LG), Peter Hicks (BG), Tony Elliot (RG), Jeff Smith (D)

PEVENSEY BROWN MELON: Chris Hardcastle (V/LG), Roger Salvetti (BG), Nick Bavin (D), Mike Durkee (?), Steve ? (?), Phil ? (?) Kelvin Jones (V?) Keef Justice & Rosie Szepanski (Lightshow)

RAMPANT: Ritchie Peters (Peter Richardson - V), Ron Hughes (LG), Dave Cawte (BG) replaced by Don Golding (BG), Mick Cooper (K), Ken Hughes (D)

REBELS: Johnny Rocco (V), Mick Reeves (G), Bryan Hatchard (D) and others

REET, PETITE & GONE: (Dave Allen (V/W'board), Stewart carr (G), Denis Reeve-Baker (G), Nick Evans (Mandolin) with Country Joe McDonald (V/G) in 2001

RENEGADES: Danny Raven (David Boltwood – V), Marc Tuddenham (aka James - G/V), Colin Wood (BG), Don Golding (G/V), Pete Light (D) replaced by Roger Standen (D) replaced by Tony Dawes (D)

RESIDENTS: Pete White (LG), Brian Baker (BG), Ray Baker (G), Colin Brimmecom (D) became Furys, then Blue Sand, then Colours

RIVALS: Ron Rickwood ("Ricky Dean"V), Rod Watts (LG), Tony Alton (G), Mick Wallis (G/V), Fred Wildsmith (BG), Roy Wells (D). Early 60s. A second, different version of the group began in the mid 60s with Grenville Mayes (V/G) and he still performs today as the One Rival.

ROADRUNNERS: Phil Shulman (V), Derek Shulman (BG), Ray Shulman (S), Ray Feast (G) 1964/5, became Simon Dupree & the Big Sound

ROSEMARY: Dave Allen (V), Steve Farrow (LG), Mick Legg (BG), John Lytle (K, G), Brian Grice (K), Dave Pittard (D)

ROYALS: Alan Lush (V), Mike Barnett (G), Nigel Kennett (BG), Rick Seamark (D), Ray Brooks (T Sax)

SAINTS SKIFFLE GROUP: Pat Green (tea chest bass) and others

SAN CELLA SOUND: Organ/drums duo Roger ? & Dave ?

SEMI-TONES: Terry Wiseman (D) and others, backed the Brook Brothers

SIMON DUPREE & the BIG SOUND: Ray Shulman (V), Derek Shulman (G), Peter O'Flaherty (BG), Eric Hine (K) replaced by Geray Kensworth, Phil Shulman (S), Tony Ransley (D) replaced by Martin Smith (MeddyEvils)

SMILING HARD: Kev Gilson (V/G/S), Andy Hamilton (V/S), Tony Gilson (BG) replaced by Nick Hug (BG) replaced by Jeremy Taner (BG), 'Spike' Edney (G/K), Dave Houghton (D), replaced by Phil Briggs (D) replaced by Larry Tolfrey (D) - one drummer replaced the other), Phil Jones (S). Late 60s, see also Blackout & Gold Dust. Edney later with Duran Duran, Queen, George Benson etc, Kev Gilson with Duran Duran, Hamilton with George Benson etc.

SONS of MAN: Ernest Yelf (V), Alan Christmas (G), Dave Yearley (BG/flute), Rod Taylor (K/V), Pete Pinckney (G), Graham Bowden (D)

SOUL SOCIETY: Phil Freeman (V), Stuart Ward (G), Doug Chalmers (BG) replaced by Mark Hunter (BG), John Davis (G/S), Mick Cooper (K) replaced by Rod Watts (K), Graham Parker/John Pratt/Alan Dodds/Kenny Hill drummers at various points. Hill also trumpet

SOUTHERN SOUNDS: Chris Ryder (V), Dave 'Digger' Hart (G), Colin Quaintance (G), Dave Field (BG), Pete St Clair (D)

SPRINGHILL: Pete Bugg (V/G), Steve Wilkins (G), replaced by Steve Farrow (G), replaced by Steve Huckle (G), Brian Grice (K), Dave Pittard (D)

ST LOUIS CHECKS: Chris West (Chris Cristodoulou – V), Billy 'Nick' Nicholson (LG), Eric 'Ginger' Merewood (K) replaced by Rod Watts (K), Mark Hunter (BG) replaced by Mick McGuigan (BG), Graham Parker (D) replaced by Alan Williams (D)

The STORMS Bernie Morley (LG), Rod Tall (RG then V) replaced (RG) by Mick Eveleigh, Alan Ordish (BG) replaced by Martin Neill (BG) then replaced by Mick Eveleigh (from RG), Paul A'Court (D) replaced by Denis Powell and then again by Paul A'Court, Len Steadall (K)

TALISMEN: Bert Parker (aka 'Billy Storm') replaced by Mick Reeves (V/G) replaced by Roger Barber (V/G), Pete Pinkney (LG), Alan Patterson (G), John Bullock (BG), Alf Pink (D) replaced by Dick Ray (D)

TANGERINE SLYDE: Bob Rose (V) replaced by Ken Cornish (V) replaced by Ian Steadman-Brown (V) possibly replaced by Chris West (V), Steve Farrow (LG), Mick Legg (BG) replaced by Mick McGuigan (BG), Brian Grice (K), Terry Threadingham (D) replaced by Steve Hollins (D)

TEAPOTS: Dave Martin (V/G), Mick Rowe (G), Phil Jones (BG), Roger Waldron (D)

THIRD DIMENSION: Marc Tuddenham (G/V), Mick McGuigan (BG), Graham Hunt (D)

THUNDERCLAPS: Dave Thistle (G/V), 'Digger' Hart (D), Pat Green (G)

TIME DYNASTY: Phil Brown (D then V) replaced on D by Alan Gordon, Nigel Shannon (BG), Pete Brown (LG), Colin Simpson (G but left). Became Hector.

TONY PORTER GROUP: Tony Porter (BG/V), Dave "Digger" Hart (LG) Dave Allaway (G/V), Les Waters (D)

TRAVIS RAYMAR: Colin Middleton (V), Bob Rose (BG) who replaced Colin Middleton as vocalist, Mick Legg replaced Bob Rose (BG), Steve Farrow (LG), Brian Grice (K), Terry Threadingham (D)

TREMORS: Personnel unknown

VOCALTONES: Vocal group: Brian Mugridge, Chris Harvey, Brian Pinhorne, Lionel haines, Jeff Forsey, Ron Dix, Alf Grainger, then quartet: Brian Mugridge, Chris Harvey, Lionel Haines, Alf Grainger

WHISKEY RIVER: Pete Bugg (V/G), Denny Barnes (LG), Rick Buckingham (BG), Bernie Fox (D)

WRONG DIRECTION: Dave Martin (V/G), Mick Rowe (G), Phil Jones (BG to Organ) then adding Rikki Cripps (BG), Roger Waldron (D)

DANCE & JAZZ BANDS – PERSONNEL:

S /A alto, T tenor, B Baritone = Saxophone, Tr = Trumpet, Tb = Trombone, Cl = Clarinet, Ban = Banjo, P = Piano, Acc = Accordion, V = Vocals, Vi = Violin, Ce = Cello, Vb = Vibraphone, G = Guitar, B = Bass, BG = Bass Guitar, Dr = Drums.

ALF HALLMAN & his ORCHESTRA: Alf Hallman (S/A, S/B, S/Soprano, Cl, Acc), John Wilkins (S/A, Cl, Tr), Bob Lawrence (S/T, S/A, Cl, Vi), Johnny Lyne (Tr, S/A), Cyril Brown (S/T, Cl, Vi), Bill Tate (Tr), George Bishop (S/B, S/A, Cl, Vi), Ted Wilcox (P, Clavioline), Roy Nightingale (B), Tommy Padmore (D)

ARTHUR WARD BAND: Arthur Ward (D), Bill Cole (P), Mike Devon (V) replaced by Mick Reeve (V) and others

BARRY McCARTHY & his DIXIELANDERS: Barry McCarthy (S/A, Cl), Doug Whitfield (Tr), Jimmy Horn (Tb) or Doug Wheeler (Tb), Doreen Nutter (P, V), Ron Blandford (B) or Stan King (B), Jack Campbell (D)

BENNY FREEDMAN ORCHESTRA: Benny Freedman (SA, Cl, Vi), Archie Horn (SA, Cl), George Hunnisett (A/S, Cl, Vi), Ernie Davis (T/S, Cl), Jack Salt (B/S, A/S, Cl), Stan Emptage (Tr), Jimmy Newton (Tr, V), Brian Barnes (P), Geoff Powell (BG, V), Ted Harvey (D)

CHIZ BISHOP QUARTET: Chiz Bishop (P, Acc), Ricky Wicheloe (A/S, Cl), Ray Lott (B), Tony Hart (D)

COMBINED THEATRES ORCHESTRA: Arthur Reed (Dir), A Beech (S/Vi), B Goodall (Vi/Tb), M Gold (Vi), H Cooper (Ce, S), R Boon (B), R Hutty (Cl, Viola), A Fotterell (Tr), S Hillier (Tb), A Hartnell (Dr), T Peaker (Vi/S), C Wakley (Vi/Tr), F Bellman (Vi), R Matthews (Ce), R Bishop (Flute), L Ferguson (Cl, S), G Cripps (Tr) P Jamieson (Tb), F Curzon (P)

GRAHAM LESLIE & HIS ORCHESTRA: Graham Leslie (P), Bob Lucas (A/S, Cl), Roy Murray (T/S, Vi), Len Farrell (T/S, Cl), Ted Chandler (Tr), , Dick Cox (Tr), Arthur Stevens (B), Tommy Thompson (D)

JOHNNY LYNE ORCHESTRA: Johnny Lyne (Arranger, S/A, Tr, Cl,), Bill Cole (P), Doug Wheeler (Tr), Arthur Ward (D) and others

KEN HOWELL ORCHESTRA: Ken Howell (Dir), Arthur Ward (D) and others

KID MARTYN BAND: Pete Dyer (Tb), Cuff Billet (Tp), Bill Greenow (Cl), Graham Patterson (P), Terry Knight (B), John Coles (Banjo)

REGINALD BANNISTRA & his MUSIC: Reginald Bannistra (D, Musical Director), Johnny Lyne (Arranger, S/A, Tr, Cl,), Les Mears (S/A, Cl), Roy Murray (S/T, Vi), Freddy Hutchins (S/A, S/B, Tr), Ken Bishop (Arranger S/T, Cl), Cyril Breeze (S/T, S/B), Ken Howell (Tr), Bob Lucas (S/A, Cl), Norman King (S/T, Cl), Dicky Cox (Tr), Stan Matthews (P) or Bob Quinton (P), Stan King (B) or Joe English (B), Arthur Ward (D), Jill Ward (V)

RON BENNETT & the CLUB QUINTET: Ron Bennett (S/T, Cl, Bass Cl), Terry Flynn (Vb, P), Bill Cole (P), George Austen (G), Nelson Peters (B), George Good (D)

ROYAL MARINES' DANCE ORCHESTRA: Roy Morgan (Bandmaster), David Elliot (AS/Cl/Vi), Leonard Spencer (TS/Cl/Vi), Jesse Palmer (BS/Flute), Jack Evans (B/P), Tom Law (D), Terrence Casselden (AS/Cl), Frank Fowler (TS/Vi), Harold Price (Tb), Tony Fitzgerald (P/Flute), Roy Morgan (Tp)

SOUTHERN COUNTIES ORCHESTRA: personnel unknown

WALLY FRY & his COLLEGIANS: Wally Fry (D), Sid Proctor (S/A, Cl, Viola), Len Farrell (S/T, Cl, Acc), Doug Wheeler (Tr), Harry Thompson (S/A, Cl), Freddy Wylie (S/T, Cl, Vi), Jock Shulman (Tr), Nobby Clark (P) Roy Beverley (B/G)

VIEUX CARRE JAZZBAND: Cuff Billet (Tp), Mick Farrier (Tb), Mac White (Cl), Frank Hurlock (Tuba), Stu Morrison (Banjo), Ken Saunders (D)

For further information please see:
http://michaelcooper.org.uk
http://www.pompeypop.co.uk/
http://pompeypop.wordpress.com/